About the author

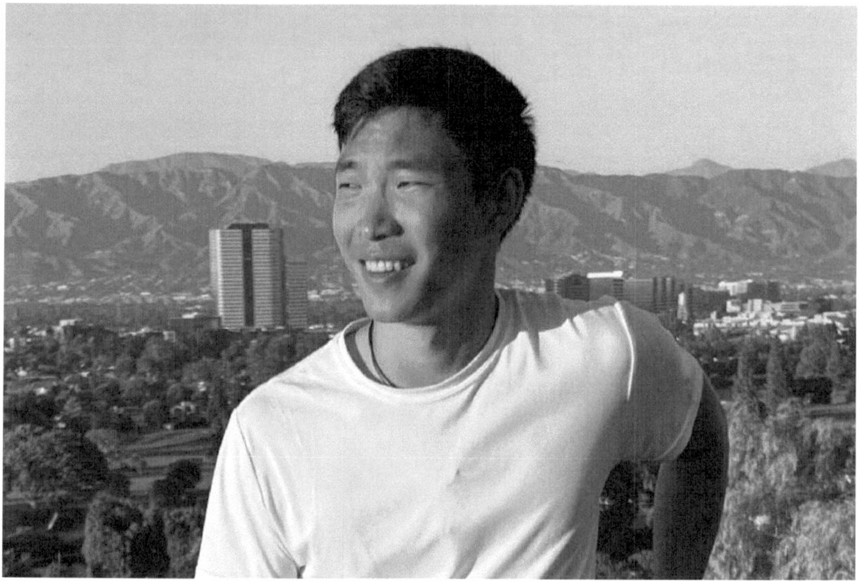

Brian H. Thai better known as *The Suit Historian* is a Canadian author and content creator living in Montreal, Canada. He is known for his series "Unknown History" which discusses the most obscure parts of history. He originally began as a Tiktoker where he eventually moved to other platforms such as Instagram and Youtube to continue his journey in shedding light into the darkest parts of history. Throughout the years, over 50 million users have watched his content!

Hence, without further ado, please enjoy the book!

This book is dedicated to my loving followers and to my mom & step-dad who always supported me no matter what.

Foreword

To my dearest fans,

Welcome to our project! For years, some of you guys have been asking for a novel to be able to keep track of all the topics I've covered and to share with all of your friends and I have the delight to tell you that it is finally done! This has been the culmination of 3 years of work and research which compiles all the knowledge I have learned throughout the years. I really hope you enjoy this book.

I, myself, hate unending introductions and forewords which is why I kept this brief and simple! Therefore, let us dive into the book and enjoy reading!

Best wishes and happy browsing!
TSH

Before you read

The pages are non-progressive, meaning that each page contains its own individual story, allowing you to leave and come back to this novel at any time. This book is designed for release to the general public and I have tried my best to make it as simple and understandable as possible! As well, many of the events of this book have **entire novels** written about them, so a lot of historical background and context is missing due to the length of each event (1-2 pages). I encourage further reading on every topic you find interesting! I sometimes link Youtube videos, documentaries, or books for some topics for you to watch/read, but I also encourage you to search up the topic yourself and read some books about it! It will provide you a lot more insight into the topic as this is simply a short introduction to it. Furthermore, this book is **not child-friendly**. This book contains various sensitive topics such as murder, rape, violence and other mature topics. Viewer discretion is advised.

(This is the last introduction page, I swear.)

So, yeah! Enjoy the book!

Warning

Author's note: Mature Content

This book delves into **intense and sensitive subject matter** that may be unsettling for some readers. It explores themes of profound violence and the harsh realities of conflict. Reader discretion is strongly advised. This content is intended for mature audiences aged 18 and older.

Chapter I:
My dear friend, the government

TW: **Mentions of sensitive topics such as torture, massacres and more** (either hidden in the embed links or in the general picture). The **content** of this **book** may not be suitable for all audiences, **viewer discretion is advised.**

Project Coast

Project Coast was a secret government initiative from 1980 to 1990 in South Africa, which aimed at eliminating the black population within the country.

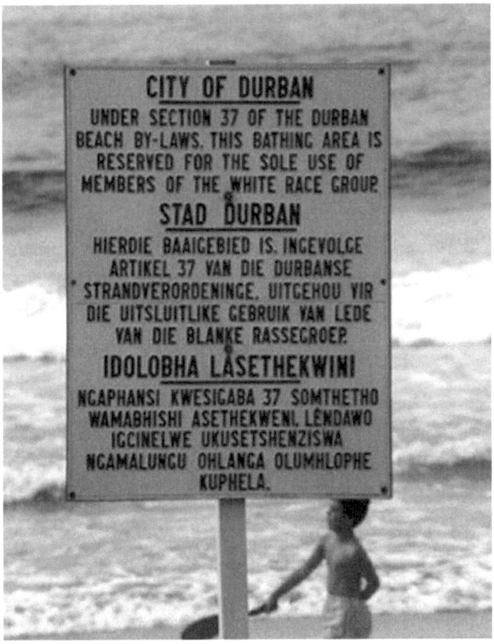

Sign that indicates that the bathing area is for "whites only"

Project Death

Project Coast was a chemical and biological weapons program (CBW) spearheaded by South African cardiologist and physician, Dr. Wouter Basson. During the *South African Border War* with Namibia, he would develop deadly neurotoxins which would be used to assassinate military officials within Namibia's rebel force, SWAPO. Additionally, the *Project* developed weaponized cholera and yellow fever, which were introduced into wells and water sources to kill local civilian and military populations. For domestic enemies, Project Coast weaponized black mamba venom, E. Coli bacteria, and investigated various incapacitating agents like

MDMA, ketamine, and tubocurarine for riot control within South Africa. In addition, the *Project* also purchased various dangerous biological agents like anthrax, salmonella, and *Clostridium perfringens* (a deadly pathogen), as well as pheromones, for potential use for crowd control.

Additionally, *Project Coast* aimed at waging racial warfare against the black population of South Africa. For this purpose, Dr. Wouter Basson would place Dr. Schalk Van Rensburg at the head of a pharmaceutical company tasked with developing a pill that would exclusively sterilize the black population. If successful, he planned to dissolve the pills in South Africa's water supply, effectively reducing the black population's birth rate without drawing international outcry.

However, Dr. Schalk Van Rensburg, who led this part of the project, failed in his efforts. He later explained to Basson that "blacks were biochemically identical to whites" and by the early 1990s, the end of *Apartheid* also meant the end of South Africa's weapons of mass destruction programs, which included *Project Coast.*

In 1997, Dr. Wouter Basson, head of the *Project,* tried to flee South Africa to escape any repercussions for his actions. However, the South African government had been tipped off by the CIA and would apprehend him with thousands of ecstasy tablets and four trunks containing details of *Project Coast*'s murder weapons and eugenics program. In October 1999, he would be indicted on 69 charges, including murder, fraud, drug trafficking, and theft. However, the case was dismissed in 2002 and today, he is still working at Mediclinic facility in the Western Cape province, causing widespread outrage among the local populace.

Project MkUltra

Project MkUltra was an illegal human brainwashing experiment by the CIA between 1953-1964.

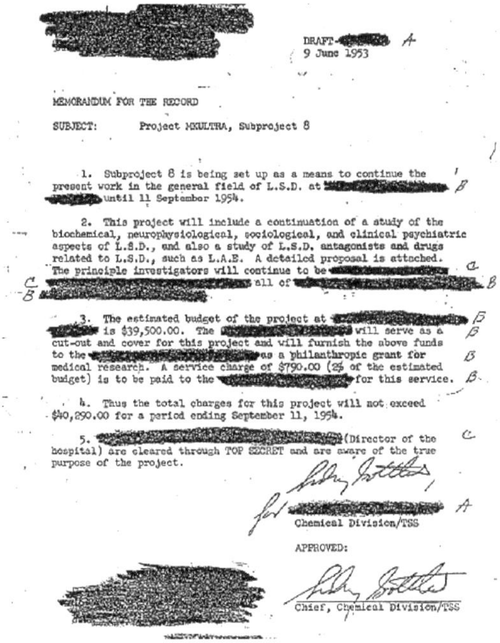

[redacted]

DRAFT-[redacted]
9 June 1953

MEMORANDUM FOR THE RECORD

SUBJECT: Project MKULTRA, Subproject 8

1. Subproject 8 is being set up as a means to continue the present work in the general field of L.S.D. at [redacted] until 11 September 1954.

2. This project will include a continuation of a study of the biochemical, neurophysiological, sociological, and clinical psychiatric aspects of L.S.D., and also a study of L.S.D. antagonists and drugs related to L.S.D., such as L.A.E. A detailed proposal is attached. The principle investigators will continue to be [redacted] all of [redacted]

3. The estimated budget of the project at [redacted] is $39,500.00. The [redacted] will serve as a cut-out and cover for this project and will furnish the above funds to the [redacted] as a philanthropic grant for medical research. A service charge of $790.00 (2% of the estimated budget) is to be paid to the [redacted] for this service.

4. Thus the total charges for this project will not exceed $40,290.00 for a period ending September 11, 1954.

5. [redacted] (Director of the hospital) are cleared through TOP SECRET and are aware of the true purpose of the project.

for [redacted]
Chemical Division/TSS

APPROVED:

[redacted]

Chief, Chemical Division/TSS

A copy of Project MkUltra after it was revealed to the public in 1975

Think like Us

In the 1950s, the CIA began a covert human experimentation program called Project MkUltra. It originated from the belief that the Chinese and Soviets had developed special drugs to brainwash American soldiers in Korea, turning them into spies for China or the Soviet Union. To counter this perceived threat, the CIA initiated its own experiments using a newly synthesized drug called lysergic acid diethylamide (LSD), which was created by Swiss chemist Albert Hoffman in 1938. Utilizing its access to numerous government institutions like prisons, schools, universities, residences, and warehouses, the CIA funded illegal brainwashing experiments on residents of these locations in an attempt to develop a brainwashing tool. The CIA also developed a "guideline" for the successful completion of these experiments, aiming to destroy one's mind to replace it with another.

One alleged case was the Harvard Experiment, in which Harvard experimented on highly talented alumni, including Ted Kaczynski, who later became a mathematics professor and eventually, a domestic terrorist known as the Unabomber. Another experiment, known as the Montreal Experiments, was conducted in Montreal, Canada, where a reputed psychiatrist, Dr. Ewen Cameron, tortured depressed students inside McGill's medical building. For years, he locked students in, injected them with paralyzing drugs, administered LSD to trigger severe hallucinations, and played pre-recorded audio tapes of their mothers telling them they hated them.

After being released, many students were unable to move and ended up in a vegetative state. Those who did walk out were nevertheless left with severe PTSD for the rest of their lives. Another case was the Atlanta Penitentiary Experiment, where prisoners were injected with vast doses of LSD and other drugs, leading to night terrors, violent hallucinations, and depression. Some prisoners even reported seeing "blood" on the walls.

Other institutions affected included the U.S. Military, Georgetown University Hospital, the Addiction Research Center in Lexington, the University of Rochester, and many others.

White Australia

The White Australia policy was a racial policy imposed in 1901 that sought to cleanse Australia of its "colored" people.

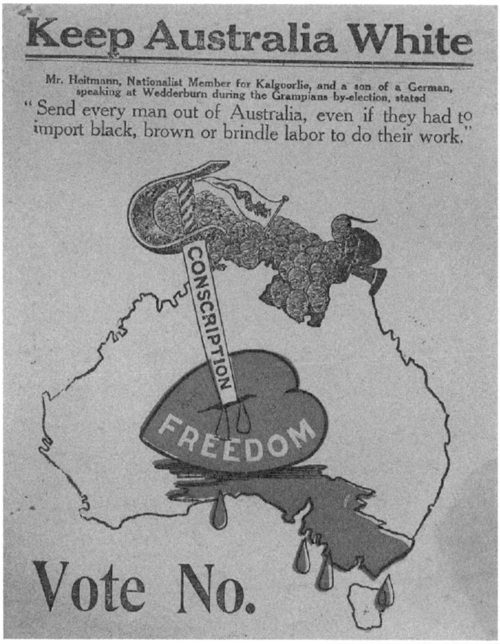

Keep Australia White poster used in the 1917 conscription

Keep Australia white

In the early 1850s, Australia began developing a wide anti-Asian sentiment due to its proximity to Asia and due to its large amounts of Asian immigration. It is in this context that legislators passed the Chinese head tax in 1855, a tax mandating a "head tax" on all Chinese immigrants in Australia and, in 1888, the *Chinese Restriction Act,* imposing harsh restrictions on Chinese immigration. In 1901, Australia became a federation and gained independence. With this new status, they began installing a new policy: *White Australia*. For the following decades, politicians would begin advocating for white supremacy and the instauration of the *Immigration Restriction Act*, which sought to enforce "being white" as a requirement for asylum in Australia. As well, legislators sought to impose measures like deportation to cleanse of Australia of its "non-white" citizenship. However, this was not done as it would have threatened their relationship with Great Britain, whose empire was predominantly non-white.

Nevertheless, on June 6, 1901, Prime Minister of Australia Edmund Barton declared that: "*We are guarding the last part of the world in which the higher ten races can live and increase freely for the higher civilization.*" Barton, like his predecessors, firmly believed that other (lesser) races were taking over Australia and would lead to its economic downfall, despite the white population accounting for 98% of Australia's population.

To instaure his policy without offending Great Britain, Barton introduced a "literacy test" which would inevitably ban many "non-whites" from the country. This was approved by Great Britain as it did not sound discriminatory. However, within Australia, he received significant criticism, with many claiming he was not radical enough and failed to protect the "*whiteness*" of Australia and had allowed "racial contamination." From that point on, racial politics became mainstream within Australia and became a popular discussion topic in journals and on the radio, where the promotion of the deportation of the "*colored*" population in Australia became normalized.

Additionally, Australia established racial extermination camps for Indigenous children, known as the *Stolen Generations*, rejected Japan's *Racial Equality Proposal* in the Treaty of Versailles, and perpetuated racial stereotypes in their media. However, by the end of World War II, the collective trauma of the war caused these racial policies to decline.

Ruby Ridge

Ruby Ridge was a failed 1992 raid by federal agents on the Weaver family, an apocalyptic family that had isolated itself from the government.

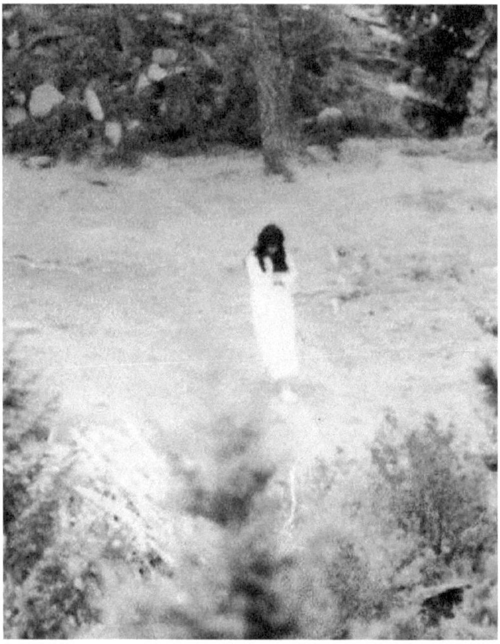

Vicki Weaver before being shot

A blatant murder?

The Weaver family was a family led by patriarch, Randy Weaver, who, alongside his family, had isolated themselves at Ruby Ridge in rural Idaho driven by their belief in an impending Armageddon that would pit Christians against an evil government force they called "*The Beast*". To fight against this force, they had stockpiled weapons in preparation for this confrontation. In 1985, Randy Weaver would join a neo-Nazi group called *The Order of the Aryan Nations,* which put him under the radar of undercover ATF agent Kenneth Fadeley who would eventually convince him to sell illegal sawed-off shotguns in 1989, leading to Weaver's arrest in 1991 and subsequent raid of his compound in 1992.

On August 21, 1992, U.S. Marshals, dressed in jungle camouflage, arrived at Ruby Ridge to arrest Weaver. They would subsequently shoot at the family's golden Labrador, Striker, barked at the agents. Hearing the shot, Randy's son, Sammy, went outside with a rifle and shot at the agents, exclaiming: *"You shot Striker, you son of a b*tch!"*. Sammy would kill an agent in a firefight and would subsequently be shot in the back after he tried to flee. As the situation escalated, a family friend on the property, Kevin Harris, retreated to the house as the FBI arrived and deployed snipers at the location. One of the most controversial shots by the FBI snipers would be attributed to specific to Lon Horiuchi, working from the sniper position *Sierra 4.*

On August 22, between 2:00 to 2:30 p.m, Lon fired a shot at Randy Weaver while he was visiting his dead son, hitting his right armpit. His second shot would hit Kevin Harris, who was running for cover, and hit Vicki Weaver *(see picture)* who was holding her 10-month-old baby, killing Vicki instantly. Eventually the raid would end when civilian negotiator and Vietnam War veteran Bo Gritz eventually convinced Randy Weaver to surrender alongside his three daughters. Weaver was later acquitted of all charges except for failure to appear in court, which led him to 16 months in prison.

Following his release he would file a $200 M civil lawsuit against the U.S. government for killing his son and his wife of which they would award him 100 000$ and $1M to his daughters to avoid the lawsuit. Prosecutor Denis Woodbury would also attempt to indict Lon Horiuchi, the FBI sniper, both during Ruby Ridge and Waco in 1997, but the case was subsequently dismissed in 2001. Today, Ruby Ridge is considered one of the most controversial interventions by U.S. federal authorities.

The Waco Siege

The Waco Siege was a failed 1993 raid by American law enforcement that resulted in over 82 deaths.

Mount Carmel on fire (1993)

Raid of Horror

In 1993, the ATF received tips that a cult known as the *Branch Davidians,* led by David Koresh, was hoarding illegal weapons and explosives. Prompted by this information, law enforcement arrived at their compound to arrest its members, but the operation went horribly wrong. The Branch Davidians were an apocalyptic cult that had separated from the Davidian Seventh Day Adventist Church and established a compound at Mount Carmel, of which they renamed it *Ranch Apocalypse.* It served as their compound of which they prepared for a possible end-of-the-world scenario. By 1988, Koresh had convinced his followers that he was a divinely appointed Messiah and King. As well, the group possessed over 8,000 rounds of ammunition, gas masks, grenades, and modified firearms converted for fully automatic fire of which could be used for the end of the world. Following this, the Bureau of Alcohol, Tobacco, and Firearms (ATF) would organize a raid on the compound, alongside other agencies like the FBI.

On February 28, 1993, ATF agents arrived in unmarked civilian vehicles and surrounded the facility. Heavily armed agents attempted to breach the compound but encountered gunfire from the Davidians, resulting in the deaths of four ATF agents and six Branch Davidians. Subsequently, the FBI assumed control of the raid, and additional forces, including the U.S. military and National Guard, were deployed. The U.S. military eventually deployed helicopters leading to continued gunfire exchange between the Davidians and the helicopters. Several ATF agents would also attempt a raid on the armory located on the roof of the compound, resulting in casualties among the agents as they were shot through walls or targeted by the Branch Davidians.

However, as the siege dragged on, the FBI became increasingly impatient. Helicopters would whir their blades at night, waking up the Davidians, loudspeakers would blast Buddhist chants, and the FBI would also employ other tactics aimed at sleep deprivation. However, on April 17th, 1993, the Attorney General of the United States authorized the use of force to breach the compound. and on that day, the FBI rammed the walls and inserted CS gas into the building.

Tragically, the CS gas ignited, causing a fire that engulfed the compound and killed 76 people, including 21 children. Following the incident, the FBI claimed that David Koresh had started the fire, while the Branch Davidians maintained that the CS gas had sparked the blaze. The failure of the Waco siege resulted in widespread distrust of American law enforcement, particularly among the right-wing in the United States. It also raised significant questions about the use of military tactics in domestic law enforcement operations.

Edgewood Human Experiments

The Edgewood experiments were a series of unethical tests by the U.S Chemical Corps between 1945-1975 conducted on misinformed United States military personnel.

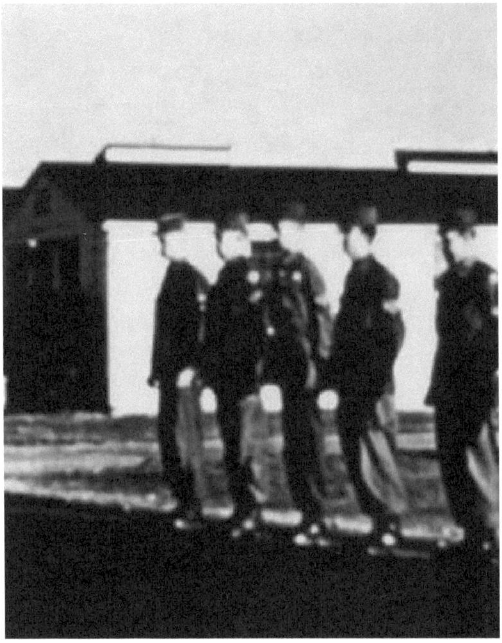

Video of Edgewood soldiers on LSD

The Experimental Trials

At the end of World War II, the U.S. Chemical Corps received a variety of chemical components from the Nazis notably tabun, soman and sarin of which they would proceed to test them on their own soldiers as a way to test out its effectiveness in military use. Its target would be Edgewood Arsenal, a remote military facility in

Maryland where soldiers would be told to sign a contract where they agreed they would help the military test out military equipment. If they refused, they would be court-martialed. In one soldier's testimony, he had originally agreed to participate in the experiment, thinking it would be a simple task like firing a mortar.

However, the doctor would inject him with *3-Quinuclidinyl benzilat*e, a powerful incapacitating agent that could cause severe hallucinations and prevent someone from performing simple tasks. He became hyperactive, started hallucinating, and was unable to focus, all behaviors noted by the doctors. As well, other soldiers were subject to nerve gas, sarin, VX, tear gas and injected LSD within their system to see the effects on the human body. As a result of this, many developed long-lasting effects, such as neurological disorders, respiratory issues, PTSD, and more. After their service was over, many participants were unable to get medical help as they did not know what drugs they were injected with and were sworn to secrecy, preventing them from revealing any classified information.

Consequently, numerous military veterans suffered for years without knowing what had happened to them and could not get any medical benefits. However, in the 1970s, information regarding the Edgewood experiments started to surface, primarily driven by investigative journalism and the efforts of concerned individuals both within and outside the government. These revelations sparked public outrage and calls for accountability.

In response to the mounting pressure, the U.S. government launched several investigations and reviews, ultimately ending the experiments in 1975. Today, multiple veterans still suffer from the effects of the experiments. A 2021 documentary titled "*Dr. Delirium and the Edgewood Experiments*" details more of the atrocities that occurred in Maryland.

United Fruits

The United Fruit Company was a banana corporation who lobbied for the overthrow of Guatemala with the U.S. government in 1959.

United Fruits company workers (1913)

A Banana Republic

Before the United Fruit Company (UFC), bananas were largely unknown to Americans and were not a staple of American breakfast culture. It would not be until the success of the United Fruits company in the 1930s that bananas quickly became associated with cereal, milk and breakfast. However, behind the scene, the UFC was engaging in various illegal and unethical schemes in Guatemala, its main source of bananas, in order to control the country and the population of bananas. For one, to force its workers to be dependent on the plantation, they would adopt a system of *debt slavery* or *debt bondage* where they would be paid via coupons. The coupons allowed them to pay for basic rent and food, but the workers had no savings and could not spend the coupons anywhere else. As well, the UFC owned a whopping 42% of the land in Guatemala as well as paying little to no taxes on the land by lying on their tax reports. Even worse, most of the land remained unused, depriving local Guatemalan farmers of livelihood opportunities.

By 1952, the Guatemalan government of newly elected leader, Jacobo Arbenz, began expropriating unused land and giving it to landless peasants which caused wide distress amongst UFC officials. In response, they began lobbying with the United States senate by declaring that communists had infiltrated the Guatemalan government and had begun seizing land within the country.

By 1954, the CIA began funding right-wing dictator Castillo Armas with planes and guns and had left him to march on the capital to overthrow Arbenz. With the army greatly demoralized by an American force who they believed they could not win against, many surrendered to Armas' force and on July 2, 1954, Arbenz would surrender and exile himself to Mexico. In response, the international community would declare this act as "economic colonialism" and condemned the coup.

Following the Armas' coup, he imprisoned various political opponents in concentration camps, outlawed labor unions, and executed over 1000 UFC workers who went against his policy. His brutal regime and subsequent assassination in 1957 would trigger a decade long civil war in 1960 between right-wing and left-wing forces called the Guatemalan Civil War, which would only be resolved in 1996, 36 years later.

Los Contras

Los Contras (The Contras) was a right-wing rebel and terrorist group in the 1980s funded by the United States government in Nicaragua.

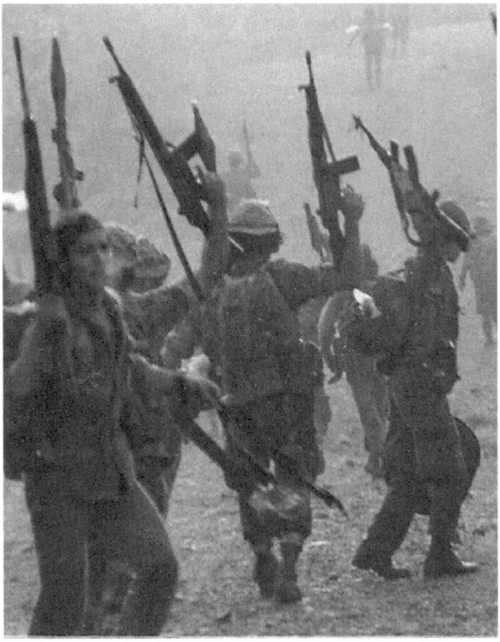

Contras soldiers (1987)

Fight Fire with Fire

In 1979, the Sandinista National Liberation Front (SNLF), a socialist political party in Nicaragua, overthrew the U.S.-backed president of Nicaragua, Anastasio Somoza, who was known for political censorship, placing his enemies in internment camps, and embezzling much of the international aid into his own pocket after the 1972 earthquake in Nicaragua. Hence, when the newly elected President of the United States, Ronald Reagan, came to power in 1981, he soon started funding a counter-revolutionary army called Los Contras. By 1982, the Contras received $31.3 million from the U.S. government, and $37.3 million in 1983.

During their time, the Contras engaged in various human rights abuses such as pillaging, massacres, and rape in multiple villages across Nicaragua. News had also spread that the Contras would make victims dig their own graves before piercing their necks with a large CIA-made bowie knife. Additionally, the Contras became heavily involved with cocaine trafficking, shipping tons of cocaine to the United States in order to purchase more weapons for the revolution. However, by 1984, support for the Contras among the American public diminished as they failed to secure any significant military success over the Sandinista government, and by 1985, the U.S. Congress had cut all financial support to the Contras. However, this had little effect on Reagan's desire to continue supporting the Contras, whom he considered "freedom fighters" for democracy.

In 1985, Ronald Reagan found a solution to bypass Congress and continue funding the Contras, known as the Iran-Contra Affair. During the affair, the U.S. brokered a deal with the terrorist group Hezbollah, which had Iranian ties. The U.S. agreed to sell weapons to Iran in exchange for the release of American hostages. During that deal, Reagan allegedly diverted over 50% of the funds to the Contras.

However, on November 6, 1986, the Lebanese newspaper Ash-Shiraa, after being tipped off by a top Iranian government official, revealed the Iran-Contra Affair, which caused a significant backlash against Reagan's presidency. Compounding the controversy was the connection between the formation of the Contras and the cartels that would later come to dominate Latin American politics for decades.

Windscale Fire

The Windscale Fire was a nuclear disaster that occurred in October 1957, which released a substantial amount of radioactive material across the United Kingdom and Europe.

Windscale Piles (1987)

Green Gas

In the mid-1940s, the United Kingdom authorized a nuclear program for the production of nuclear weapons, which included the establishment of facilities at Windscale near the west coast of England. By 1951, Windscale had two nuclear reactors with graphite moderators, heated to around 250 degrees Celsius to produce plutonium for the production of nuclear weapons. However, in 1957, a routine check-up turned into a disaster.

On October 9, 1957, one of the graphite reactors reached 400 degrees Celsius (150 degrees hotter than usual) which prompted the staff to attempt to cool it down using fans. However, by October 11, 1957, the reactor burst into flames and expelled radioactive substances into the air. Operators made multiple attempts to cool the pile down, including an attempt using carbon dioxide as a coolant at 4:30 a.m., followed by water hoses at 800 gallons a minute by 8:55 a.m., and eventually at 1000 gallons a minute by 12 p.m, which eventually extinguished the fire. However, the radioactive substances had already spread into the air. Soon, they reached the city of Harrow in Great Britain, Antwerp and Mol in Belgium, and Essen in Germany. This spread of radioactive gases would eventually result in 240 additional cancer cases that year, with 100 of those being fatal. Additionally, the contamination extended to the milk in the area, leading to its systematic disposal.

In response, the UK government began censoring the media about the event and downplaying the severity of it. Journalists were restricted from reporting on the full extent of the radiation release, and information about the health risks posed by the incident was suppressed. This censorship continued for years after the disaster, with the government maintaining tight control over information related to nuclear energy and its potential hazards. The government would eventually acknowledge and investigate it in 1988 under the *"Penny Report"*.

However, even though the event was downplayed, many became increasingly against the government's policy to test potential nuclear weapons in the United Kingdom. Today, because of the multiple nuclear disasters in history (Fukushima, Chernobyl, etc.), many in modern times are reluctant to adopt nuclear energy despite its clear benefits (clean energy, renewable and non-polluting)

Project Eldest Son

Project Eldest Son was a covert plan by U.S. Studies and Observations Group (SOG) during the Vietnam War to introduce defective munitions into Vietcong supplies as a form of psychological warfare.

AK 47 ammunition piles

Trapped ammunition

In 1965, the Military Assistance Command–Studies and Observation Group (SOG) was given a peculiar task: to sabotage Vietcong ammunition supplies in order to create mass paranoia among the troops. This was done via the CIA's Okinawa lab, which manufactured 7.62 mm ammunition for Russian AK-47s, which would explode when fired. These defective rounds were then shipped to SOG headquarters in Vietnam, where operatives would substitute the ammunition they found with the tampered ones. By the fall of 1965, every SOG personnel carried a tampered magazine containing at least one Eldest Son round, which would explode when fired. They would replace a downed Viet Cong soldier's magazine with an Eldest Son magazine, hoping the enemy would loot their own soldiers for ammunition. Additionally, the CIA manufactured defective communist mortar rounds which SOG operatives would place near enemy bases.

By 1967, the SOG team had expanded operations into Laos. There, they constructed fake bunkers filled with Eldest Son ammunition which would lead Vietcong soldiers to unknowingly collect malfunctioning ammunition from these bunkers. This time, these defective rounds were designed to be particularly deadly; they would often cause the weapon to explode and injure/kill the user.

In the spring of 1968, the effectiveness of this new bullet was reportedly confirmed when the 101st Airborne Division found a communist soldier holding his exploded AK-47 with the bolt blown back, with the Eldest Son round having entered his skull, killing him instantly. However, Project Eldest Son was not without its disadvantages. In November 1968, an American helicopter carrying CIA-manufactured *Eldest Son* rounds was struck by Vietcong artillery, which caused the ammunition to explode, killing everyone on board.

However, the project would eventually end in 1969 after an American news media would reveal the extent of the program, which compromised the project and caused the communist forces to stop looting dead soldiers. After the revelation, the SOG eventually ended the program and continued with their regular tasks for the remainder of the war.

My Lai Massacre

The My Lai Massacre was a mass killing of 504 villagers by the U.S. Army in the small village of My Lai in Vietnam.

Vietnamese women and children in Mỹ Lai before being killed in the massacre.

Senseless killings

On the morning of March 16, 1968, villagers in My Lai were starting their day, cooking rice for breakfast and slowly waking up when they were suddenly interrupted by hundreds of American GIs, believing they were engaging the 48th Viet Cong Battalion. Observing the unusual scene, some soldiers began bayoneting civilians and shooting them indiscriminately. In panic, a group of 15-20 villagers, seeking refuge and protection, went to the temple with incense to pray for help, but were shot in the head by soldiers. Elsewhere, soldiers rounded up groups of people—mostly women, children, and elders—and gunned them down in ditches, leaving their bodies to rot.

Meanwhile, many women in the village tried to shield their children, pleading that they were not Viet Cong, but were shot regardless and then their children, attempting to flee after their mothers were killed, were also gunned down. Numerous cases of rape were also documented, including a horrific incident where a soldier shot a woman's children before raping and killing her. The soldiers also burned down the village, slaughtered livestock, destroyed religious temples and fired upon groups of civilians with grenade launchers, leading to even more casualties. The GIs would only face one casualty—a soldier who shot himself in the foot to avoid participating in the massacre. After the massacre, the military falsely reported that 128 Viet Cong and only 28 civilians were killed in a brutal firefight.

The American military magazine *Stars and Stripes* relayed this fabricated account, celebrating the supposed victory. However, in March 1969, a year later, ex-GI Ronald Ridenhour officially reported the incident to the Pentagon. Ridenhour also contacted Seymour Hersh, a journalist for the New York Times whose article and accompanying photographs of the massacre shocked the American public and contributed significantly to growing disapproval of the Vietnam War. The revelation of the My Lai Massacre and its subsequent cover-up prompted widespread outrage and led to an official investigation.

Eventually, Lieutenant William Calley, one of the key figures in the massacre, was convicted of mass-murder. Calley was sentenced to life imprisonment, but his sentence was later reduced to 20 years, and he served only a few years of it under house arrest before being released.

MOVE Bombings

The MOVE Bombings were a series of bombings in 1985 committed by the Philadelphia police against Black activist group, MOVE.

MOVE bombings aftermath

A bombing against Philadelphia

MOVE was an African-American communal group known for its anti-establishment and anti-technology stance. Members of MOVE rejected Western medicine and clothing, refused to use toilets and turned their backyard into a landfill instead of disposing of garbage through the city. In the 1970s, they were vocal activists against zoos, pet stores, and other institutions that they believed were harmful to society. As a result, many members were arrested for their protests, filling Philadelphia's jail cells. In 1976, the Philadelphia Police Department (PPD), upon realizing these individuals were part of the same group, began to monitor

MOVE around the clock. In March 1976, MOVE members were celebrating the release of their friends from prison when a neighbor called the police to complain about the noise. When the PPD arrived, a member allegedly threw a brick at the police, prompting the officers to respond with batons, beating multiple members of the group.

During the altercation, an officer pushed Janine Africa to the ground and stomped her unconscious while she was holding her baby. The child's skull was crushed and he died instantly.

> *"The murder of my children, my family, will always affect me, but not in a bad way. When I think about what this system has done to me [...] it makes me even more committed to my belief,"*

That night, the murder of Janine Africa's child would radicalize the group forever.

Between 1977 and 1978, MOVE placed fake bombs in several hotels across Philadelphia to warn that they would strike for real if the police didn't stop harassing them and in 1978, they were forced to relocate to a new area after attempting to convince their neighbors to join their cause. Upon moving, they armed themselves in their new residence and barricaded themselves to protect against anticipated police actions. By 1983, the police had grown tired of MOVE as they had resorted to using loudspeakers to harass their neighbors, hoping to pressure the mayor into releasing imprisoned members.

By 1985, the mayor of Philadelphia would finally approve a raid against them. On May 13, 1985, the Philadelphia Police fired over 10,000 rounds of ammunition at the MOVE house and a police helicopter dropped a C4 explosive on the house, killing 11 people inside, including five children. The raid was ultimately a failure destroying 61 homes and leaving over 250 people homeless.

Residential School System

The Residential School System was a system of boarding schools enforced by the Canadian government between 1892 and 1950.

Residential School in Fort Resolution, Canada

Forgetting your culture

In 1892, it was the beginning of the school year for Canada's residential school system for indigenous children. As part of the initiative, the government had threatened reservations to stop giving them rations unless they send their kids to residential school. Under the threat of starvation, over 4000 children would be sent to school, a number that would only increase with time. Inside these schools, they were subject to various amounts of torture and abuse in order to assimilate the children. One testimony explained that when she had tried to speak her native language with other kids in the school, her tongue was scrubbed using a steel wool sponge making her tongue bleed, leaving her crying in front of her classmates. As well, teachers would also lock children in broom closets for misbehaving or if they refused to renounce their religion or culture. In one case, a child who had tried to flee the residential school was brought in front of everyone before getting beaten down and tortured by adult members of the staff. As well, residential schools were dirty and untidy and illness spread rapidly within the schools.

Children, especially young girls, were often subject to rape by the school priests who would enter their common rooms at will. School inspectors who reported on the horrid conditions of the schools were often ignored or silenced, leaving the system in place for decades. In 1902, a child by the name of Johnny Sticks was found in a forest near the school. His body had been frozen and parts of his face were chewed off by wild animals. He had escaped conditions so horrifying that he had preferred to freeze to death than to return to the school.

However, Johnny was not the only one to die within residential schools, over 6000 children would die either from spreading disease, malnutrition, physical abuse or accidents. By 1920, school inspectors would remark that the school was "not like other boarding schools" as the face of the children seemed to look particularly depressed, seemed to miss any desire to live and missed amicable interactions between kids like other schools.

By the 1950s, the schools would close due to growing public awareness and controversy, but would also lead to alternate ways of assimilation like the 60s scoop ("see 60s Scoop")

60s Scoop

The 60s Scoop was a mass-kidnapping of over 20 000 indigenous children by the Canadian government between 1960-1980.

The Mohawk Institute residential school

Where is my mother?

By the 1960s, the number of indigenous children within Canada's *Indian residential school system* diminished. As a solution, Canada began its 60s scoop policy, which sought to assimilate indigenous peoples by "teaching" them Euro-Canadian and Christian values. To do this, social services would often take away indigenous children under the pretext of family poverty, abuse or inadequate care and send them into a white family. However, this was not always the case. On the case of Tauni Sheldon, an indigenous child, she was taken straight from the hospital in March 1970 after she was born in a small hospital in Thunder Bay, Ontario.

"Today's child: Helen Allen. She is the first-ever Eskimo baby to arrive at Today's Child. (...) She is a content little baby who eats and sleeps well and is not all demanding. A sober little (...)".

This was a newspaper clipping, seven months after she was taken away by Canada's social services, which changed her name to "Hellen Allen". A couple of months later, she was adopted into a white family. However, despite her adoptive mother being very loving and caring, Tauni (or Helen) always felt empty, like something was missing. At school, she was extremely reclusive and experienced severe bullying. In one instance, white boys held her head and painted her face with white-out, telling her she should become white.

As a result, she deeply resented being Indigenous and always tried to become as white as possible. She had totally lost touch with herself and her culture.

Winnipeg, 1993.

23 years later, in 1993, Tauni would eventually find her biological mother and offer to meet her at the Winnipeg airport. When they met, they hugged deeply, with her mom holding flowers. She still had not processed the 23 years where her baby had disappeared from the hospital.

Throughout the years, it is not just Tauni that had to face the 60s scoop, but rather over 20,000 children who were scooped and abducted by the Canadian government, some of which will never get to know or see their biological parents ever again.

Blackwater Incident

The Blackwater Incident was a massacre of 17 Iraqis civilians by *Blackwater Co.*, a private military contractor (PMC)

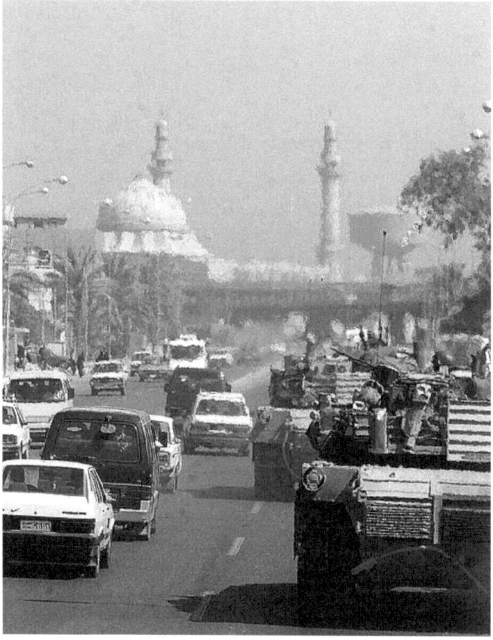

U.S. convoys in Baghdad

A deadly massacre

In August 2003, *Blackwater Co.*, a private military contractor, received a $ 21M contract from the U.S. Government as a security detachment, but on September 16, 2007, the company would massacre 17 Iraqi civilians in broad daylight.

On that fateful day, a Blackwater convoy fired on civilians in the middle of Nisour Square, Iraq, which resulted in 17 deaths and 20 injuries. What truly happened that day is unclear. One of the testimonies of the massacre was by Iraqi policemen, Khalaf Salman. On that day, he describes seeing four heavily armed Blackwater tanks entering Nisour Square, driving erratically to then make a sharp U-turn in Nisour Square before coming to an abrupt stop in the middle of the intersection. There, the soldiers within the tank fired upon a white Kia, killing the student and the mother inside instantly. What sustained after was allegedly "random" gunfire for the next 15 minutes as the soldiers began massacring civilians. In response, according to Blackwater's testimony, on that day, a white Kia approached the Blackwater convoy and had refused to stop despite warnings like bottles thrown on the vehicle, verbal warnings or a warning shot of which the convoy acted in "self-defense" by firing at the vehicle killing the student and the mother. Then, the convoy that would announce that they were under-attack by Iraqi police and insurgents dressed in civilian clothing and began firing at the convoy, which resulted in a firefight.

On October 2, 2007, the Investigative Committee of the United States House of Representatives proclaimed that Blackwater guards had used deadly force on a weekly basis and always fired first in 80% of all encounters. As well, on October 4, the Committee had indicated that Blackwater had fired without provocation and that none of the civilians were armed. It also declared that none of the Iraqi policemen had fired at the convoy.

On October 13, 2007, the FBI declared that the convoy had used excessive force, with only the two passengers of the white Sedan being justifiable for fear of bodily harm. In December 2008, five of the soldiers were charged with manslaughter, resulting in four of the men being convicted in 2014.

Unit 731

Unit 731 was a covert biological weapons unit which engaged in unethical human experimentation and biological weapons development between 1937-1945.

Unit 731's Headquarters (1937)

Kamo Detachment

In 1931, the Empire of Japan took over Manchuria and began a covert biological weapons operation inside the *Zhongma fortress* in Harbin. Inside, the prisoners were repeatedly tortured and injected with all sorts of biological agents, like anthrax or the plague. However, in 1937, they began a more serious project under Unit 731 to test for feasible biological weapons to use against China. Under it, they brought prisoners all across China and deposited them into a test center (see picture) as human guinea pigs. In the facility, the Japanese tested biological agents on civilians where they were injected with illnesses and left to die in a prison cell.

As well, prisoners were forced into artificial freezers where they were frozen and thawed out, which caused blisters and eventually, death. Prisoners were also dissected alive so that scientists could see the insides of the human body after being exposed to biological agents.

As well, in the efforts of developing a biological weapon against the Chinese, the Japanese would also lead hundreds of prisoners to a field and bomb them using biological weapons to see the effects on the human body. These prisoners were often regular everyday people like carpenters, farmers or blacksmiths who were captured from their villages to be experimented on. By 1940, Unit 731 would also carry out a biological attack on civilians called the *Kaimingjie Germ Attack*. On August 3, 1940, a plague-laden Unit 731 train departed for Ningbo carrying planes which dropped grains carrying plague ridden fleas which were dropped on the busy Kaimingjie street.

Hundreds of people would die and the street would be burned down to protect the rest of the civilians in Ningo. Soon, these types of attacks would be common and would continue until the end of the war. After the war, many of the people responsible for Unit 731 would be tried at the Tokyo War Crimes Trial in 1946. However, Shiro Ishii, the head of Unit 731, would be exempt from the trial and would be protected by the United States as part of *Operation Paperclip*.

He would die peacefully at age 67 in 1959, never having answered for his crimes.

Operation Paperclip

Operation Paperclip was a United States operation between 1945-1949 to bring thousands of Nazi scientists to the United States following the end of World War 2.

V2 Rocket

All for science

Following the end of World War II (1939-1945), the Allied countries began the *Nuremberg Trials* against Nazi Germany for their atrocities during WW2, including mass-slaughter, genocide and crimes against humanity. However, the United States developed the idea to hire Nazi scientists who were on trial to advance their own scientific programs as well as to prevent them from joining the Soviet Union. As part of the deal, the United States would shield them from the Nuremberg Trials in exchange for their help.

One of these scientists was named Herbert Wagner, who during WWII, served as a scientist under Nazi Germany and developed the guided H-293 bombs which set out to have caused devastating damage against the Allies between 1943-1945. As part of the deal, he would also avoid trial in Nuremberg and sent to help the United States in Fort Detrick, Maryland to develop similar weapons for the U.S. Army.

Another notable member was Wernher Von Braun, a rocket scientist who helped the Nazis develop their V2 ballistic missiles which killed thousands in London. As well, he was complicit in genocide, leading thousands to die in concentration camps in an effort to build his rockets. As part of the same deal, he would soon arrive in Fort Bliss, Texas and begin his career as a rocket scientist in the United States and become the director of NASA in 1960 despite his past as an officer of Hitler's *Schutzstaffel* (SS). Another criminal as part of the deal was Otto Ambros, a German chemist who had developed chemical weapons like sarin gas, tabun as well as engaged in slave labor and unethical testing chemical gas on prisoners.

He was subsequently tried and convicted in the Nuremberg Trials for mass-murder and slavery, but was subsequently received a job by the United States after he was freed in 1951 and went to work for the chemical company W.R. Grace and later the U.S. the Department of Energy. As well, one of the most cruel men to be accepted into the program, SS-*Brigadeführer* Walter Schieber. During his time with the Nazis, he had tortured 150 prisoners by replacing their food with an artificial paste made from old cloth and clothing, of which 116 prisoners died in his experiment. However, in 1947, he was recruited by the United States and ended up working for the U.S. Chemical Corps.

These are just a couple of the thousands of war criminals accepted into the United States and left a long-standing taint in the American legacy across the world.

Nazi Gas Wagons

Nazi Gas Wagons were mobile devices used to execute Jews, Poles, Romani people by the Nazi Regime between 1939-1945

Possible Nazi Gas Wagon (1940)

Portable Death

In 1941, chief of SS, Heinrich Himmler, witnessed a mass-execution of Jews in Minsk. Upon seeing the scene, he vomited and was horrified and asked Arthur Nebbe, one of the main perpetrators of the Holocaust, to develop alternative ways to kill his victims. From it, Nebbe could develop a van that could transport patients and kill them during transport. These vehicles were called *Spezialwagen* ("special wagon"). The first victims of the wagons were Soviet mental patients who were placed into the vans and killed. From then, gas vans were widely used in Germany and its occupying territories to kill Jews, Poles, Soviets and Romani people that the Nazis deemed to be a threat to the *"Aryan race"*. The vans would also be disguised as *"Kaiser's Coffee Shop"*, a cover-up front for the true purpose of the vehicle. In the U.S.S.R., the vans would earn the reputation of the *Soul Killer*, driving fear into anyone who heard of the vehicle. By 1940, they had driven to mental health hospitals and executed patients that they deemed mentally unwell ("see Aktion T4"). As well, the majority of the killings were done by wagons in the Chełmno extermination camp in order to mass-murder patients who were brought there. When activated, the truck would expel carbon dioxide into the inside of the truck, suffocating the inmates inside, who would often scream for help and beg the Germans to let them out while hitting at the walls of the car. The aftermath of the wagons was often blue-colored bodies, a leftover of excrements and sweat and a traumatizing scene for any officer tasked on cleaning it. As a result, the Germans designed Zyklon B, a cyanide-based pesticide that would kill the inmates faster, of which the Nazis prided themselves in being "humane" killers. By the end of 1942, over 20-30 death vans were produced by the Nazis, but they soon went out of favor after the usage of gas chambers as the primary mode of execution for inmates.

Today, Nazi Death Wagons has left a legacy on the human consciousness, as humanity reflects on the atrocities it is able to impose on each other, simply on the basis of race or religion.

Project Babylon

Project Babylon was a space gun project developed by the Iraqi government until 1990.

Piece of Hussein's Babylon supergun

Death Ray

On March 22 of 1990, Gerard Bull, the main architect of Saddam Hussein's *Project Babylon*, was shot three times in the head at point-blank in his apartment in Brussels. Previously, his apartment has been broken-in multiple times as a warning before he was assassinated. Amongst the suspects were the American CIA, the Israeli Mossad or British MI6, who all felt threatened with Iraq possibly developing a super weapon. The idea for a super weapon had been seen a long time ago with Project HARP, a joint project in the 1950s between the United

States and Canada to develop high-altitude projectile weapons who would fire projectiles into space before re-entering the atmosphere and hitting the target.

The head of the project was a certain Gerard Bull who believed super-guns were the way of the future and could help launch satellites without using rockets which would be much more cost efficient. To set up the project, Bull installed an 8.9 meters HARP cannon and fired over 100 rockets into the ionosphere from Barbados. However, due to increasing bureaucratic pressure and immense opposition, his project would eventually end, devastatingly he was never able to complete his goal. Following that, Bull would eventually begin selling arms to South Africa who were under arms embargo in the United States at the time, which would lead Bull to prison for six months. Following this event, Bull felt heavily ostracized from the West and began finding new sources of funding to help him accomplish his lifelong dream of building a supergun. One of these people was Saddam Hussein, then the Secretary of Defence of Iraq. For the first time, Bull was granted sufficient funding ($25 M) for his weapon and was viewed highly in Iraq, granting him prestige and recognition.

At the time, Iraq was also the perfect choice as they were not seen as an enemy country to the United States and simply wanted to be a leader in the Arab world. Under the project, Bull would order multiple parts of the super-gun all across the world, disguising them as pipes, pieces or different sewage parts. The first parts of the project was called "Baby Babylon" of which small problems would be revealed by it. However, before Bull was able to fix the problems, he would be assassinated in his apartment in Brussels, leaving his legacy unfinished.

Shortly after, parts of the super-gun were seized at UK customs and projects for the 100 feet super-guns were never completed.

Operation CONDOR

Operation Condor was a U.S.-backed coup in multiple Latin American countries from 1975 to 1983 under the pretext of vanquishing the region from communism, which transformed the region into a puppet continent for the United States.

Declassified CIA picture of Jorge Rafael Videla

Condor by country

Argentina: Isabel Perón, the first female head of state of Argentina, was elected after her husband, Juan Perón, died. She continued his work in social reforms until she was overthrown in a military coup in 1976 by U.S.-backed Jorge Rafael Videla. Under Videla's reign, right-wing policies, such as the privatization of medical services and other public enterprises, caused widespread poverty. He also enforced disappearances of his enemies and operated torture camps. During Argentina's 1978 World Cup, torture camps were still operating a couple of miles from the stadium, and people inside the camps could hear the sounds of cheering from outside.

Brazil: João Goulart, a young countryman, was elected president of Brazil in 1961. However, his presidency ended in 1964 after a U.S.-backed coup.

Bolivia: Juan José Torres fled to Argentina in 1971 after a U.S.-backed coup in Bolivia. He was killed by Videla's death squads in Argentina in 1976.

Uruguay: The President of Uruguay, Juan Bordaberry, surrendered and agreed to all conditions of the military in 1973, beginning the military dictatorship.

Chile: Salvador Allende, after promising to give unused land to peasants, was overthrown by Augusto Pinochet, a U.S.-trained dictator. It is suspected that the massive banana conglomerate, the United Fruit Company, lobbied with the U.S. government due to fears that Allende would expropriate their land.

Peru: Francisco Morales Bermúdez overthrew the government in a successful coup in 1975.

Paraguay: Alfredo Stroessner overthrew the government of Paraguay in 1954, establishing a military dictatorship. His brutality would be revealed years later in the *Archives of Terror*.

Charbonneau Commission

The Charbonneau Commission was a 2011 public inquiry into interference between organized crime and construction in the Province of Quebec, Canada.

FBI Agent, Joseph Pistone

A shocking discovery

In 2011, the Canadian government under Jean Charest led a public investigation into construction companies within the small province of Quebec, also known as *La Belle Province*. Over the years, Quebec has gotten into the Quiet Revolution and had revolutionized its industries and healthcare, but within it, rumors circulated that the construction system was heavily corrupt with some contracts being distributed to the organized crime families. It is in this context that Supreme Court justice, Justine Charbonneau, would oversee 300 witnesses from independent contractors, former mayors, engineers and even undercover FBI agent Joseph Pistone. One of the star witnesses of the investigation was construction boss, Lino Zambito, of which he would admit that his company engaged in cartel practices of which it paid off the mob, rigged bids for public contract works and lied about expenses to obtain more money from the government. He would also admit to having paid 2.5% of his profits to the mayor of the city in order to keep his favorable contracts.

As well, another witness, Nathalie Normandeau, a former Liberal party cabinet minister, who was also accused of corruption as Zambito had admitted to buying her multiple concert tickets and helping her organize her political campaign. In exchange, she would overrule senior officers in awarding public works contracts to various different companies. However, unlike Zambito, these allegations have not yet been proven in court. Another key member was Tony Accurso, who within his luxury yacht, *The Touch*, hosted various parties of which he allegedly took advantage to secure contracts for his firms.

Alongside him was also Nicolo Milioto, also known as "Mr. Sidewalk" who was famously caught by CCTV on a sidewalk handing a former mob boss, Nick Rizzuto Jr, the Patriarch of the Rizzuto crime family, a sock filled with cash. As well, final information was revealed by a whistle-blower, Ken Pereira, who, after searching into the construction union officers (the FTQ), who would find astronomical expenses. However, before he had time to report the incident, he would be offered 300 000$ by the FTQ as well as threatened by the Montreal Mob.

Today, despite the investigations, it is still an ongoing issue and does not seem it will resolve anytime soon...

Abduction of the Panchen Lama

The abduction of the Panchen Lama was a kidnapping in 1989 by the Chinese government of the 11th Panchen Lama, Gedun Chokyi Nyima.

Potala palace, Tibet

End of the cycle

On May 14, 1995, the Dalai Lama of Tibet announced the next Panchen Lama as Gedhun Choekyi Nyima, who was only six at the time. This announcement was particularly important for Tibetans, as the Panchen Lama is a figure that is responsible for seeking for the next Dalai Lama as well as second in authority to him.

However, just five days later, Gedhun vanished without a trace. As well, his parents also disappeared just a couple of days later. Two days after Gedhun's disappearance, Jadrel Rinpoche, head of the Panchen Lama search committee, also disappeared after being accused of treason by the Chinese government of which five days later, Chinese officials arrived in Tibet with another boy, Sengchen Lobsang Gyaltsen, whom they proclaimed as the Panchen Lama. Sengchen's rule was met with widespread refusal from most Tibetans, who suspected foul play. He was closely surveilled by the Chinese Communist Party, restricted in his movements, and denied access to the internet. Currently residing in Beijing, he rarely visits Tibet. When questioned about Gedhun whereabouts, the Chinese government claimed he was safe and undergoing studies, but provided no further details.

As of May 19, 2020, the Chinese government has proclaimed that he is "*now a college graduate with a stable job*". However, the political purpose of this alleged kidnapping is clear. The Panchen Lama and the Dalai Lama both have very important roles in Tibetan politics, hence, by establishing their own successor, they would be able to control the Tibetan government. Even today, his kidnapping is still grieved by Tibetan communities around the world.

London, United Kingdom, 2019

A group of Tibetans reunite in a small building in London. For the anniversary of the Panchen Lama, an artist had reconstructed a picture of what the Panchen Lama should look like now. It can now be found on the website of *FreeTibet.org*. His picture today is commemorated by the Tibetan community and many refuse to acknowledge the one imposed by the CCP.

World Cup

The 1978 Argentina World Cup was a controversial FIFA tournament hosted by the Argentinian military junta, which tortured prisoners near the stadium.

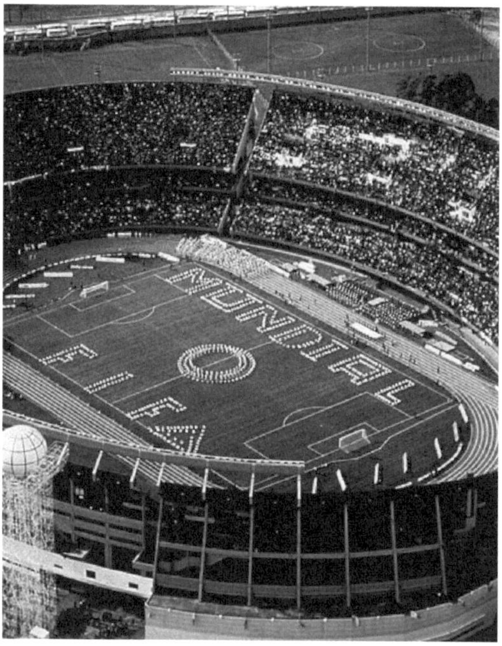

Estadio Monumental, 1978

A blood filled cup

In 1976, the United States government overthrew the democratic government of Argentina under Juan Perón (see *Operation Condor*), replacing it with a right-wing military dictatorship. During its reign, the military enforced disappearances, tortured political opponents and threw people out of planes into the ocean to make them "disappear". These people were known as *los desaparecidos* or known as "The Disappeared". Despite these severe human rights violations, FIFA, the international body for soccer (or football), announced in 1978 that the next World Cup would be held in Argentina. This led to international outcry as the country's ongoing human rights abuses were widely known, which also laid outcry against the United States who had vouched for Argentina during the FIFA vouching bids.

In response, Henry Kissinger, the United States Secretary of State, sent a memo to Argentinian general and de facto leader Rafael Videla, stating that "if there were things to be done, they should be done quickly." Nevertheless, despite the international outcry, the World Cup was hosted, anyway. In 1978, the tournament took place at the *Estadio Monumental*, mere blocks away from the military junta's torture camp, the ESMA (Escuela Mecánica de la Armada), a former mechanics school converted into a torture center. During the World Cup, the leaders of the military junta were determined to renew Argentina's image, convinced that hosting it would help counter the widespread criticism.

However, despite this desire, the military junta continued its enforced disappearances, which was the case of Lilianna Pellegrino, a 21-year-old human rights activist who, on November 28, 1978, was kidnapped by the junta in front of her home. Her husband, Carlos, was also met by large unmarked vehicles of which he was brutally beaten by multiple men before being taken to the ESMA by junta associates. During the World Cup, they were tortured using rods, waterboarding, forced humiliation and used as punching bags while the World Cup matches continued. They were also deprived of food, deprived of water, kept in filthy chambers, kicked in the head, and electrocuted for information. Inside, they could hear spectators cheering as Argentina scored.

On June 28, 1978, a final roar resonated in *Buenos Aires*, prompting the ESMA director to kiss the inmates and tell them, "We won! We won!"

Black Ships

Black Ships were Western vessels in the 16th to 17th century that forced Japan to open its economy through "gunboat diplomacy".

Japanese painting of a black ship (17th century)

Black Ships

For over 214 years, Japan followed the policy of Sakoku (鎖国) which allowed limited connections with the Western world. However, in 1853, American Black ships would change the course of Japanese history. In July 1853, Admiral Matthew Perry arrived in Japan with his fleet of powerful coal-powered boats painted in complete black with the intention of opening its economy. The Japanese, who had never seen a coal-powered boat before, were terrified. Upon arriving at the coast of Uraga, Japanese ships surrounded Matthew Perry's convoy to greet the admiral. Perry then yelled at the ships, telling them he was there to deliver a letter to the emperor. In response, the officials told him to go to Nagasaki for foreign business. He responded that

"If I was not allowed to port, I will sail directly to Edo and burn it to the ground."

In response, officials allowed him to enter Japan, making him the first American to set foot in Japanese soil. After delivering his letter, he left Japan, only to return the next year with twice the military power and eight fearsome Black ships. This time, he proclaimed that he would not leave until he got a treaty. By then, the Americans had successfully terrified the Japanese, and the Shogun accepted the signing treaty, which ended its isolationist policy and opened trade to American and Western trade.

By 1858, the United States would sign the Harris Treaty, the final treaty, granting favorable trading conditions to the United States. Following it, Japan would open its doors to Western powers which deeply westernized and industrialized Japan engaging the Meiji revolution. With it came Western styled uniforms, bars, coffee shops and a much more powerful military. It would also lead Japan into a path of self-destruction as its perceived superior Westernization to other Asian countries would lead it to develop a superiority complex becoming one of the reasons for Japan's later conquest of Asia during World War II.

During the war, it terrorized not only its East and Southeast Asia neighbors, but also the United States, who had begun its rise to power in the first place, leaving a lasting legacy in world history.

Operation Fishbowl

Operation Fishbowl was a U.S. government nuclear experiment which detonated several high-altitude thermonuclear bombs over Johnston Atoll between 1953-1962.

Operation Starfish Prime seen from Hawaii

Seeing the sun

In 1962, the U.S. began a series of high-altitude nuclear tests over the Pacific in a period of high tension between the United States and the Soviet Union. On June 2, 1962, the first bomb codenamed Bluegill was launched but was subsequently lost and was forced to self-destruct. The second bomb codenamed Starfish, also failed as the missile tore itself apart. However, on July 9th, 1962, the third bomb, codenamed Starfish Prime, succeeded. However, the explosion was more powerful than expected. In Hawaii, the nearest populated area near the explosion, over 2000 streetlights, vast electrical damage was seen, and set off multiple burglar alarms. As far as New Zealand, many have claimed to see a flash of new light within the sky from the direction of the explosion. The explosion also downed over six satellites, left a permanent radioactive belt in the atmosphere and permanently shut down three other satellites.

However, despite its negative effects on both the environment and the civilian population, the United States continued the program. On July 25 of 1962, the United States planned to send another nuclear missile, this time codenamed Bluefish Prime, but the attempt was a failure and the bomb had to self-destruct. The project was soon abandoned. However, a couple of months later, scientists, frustrated they were unable to launch Bluefish, tried again, this time under the name Bluegill Double Prime, it was a failure again.

On October 25, 1962, the team tried one last time with Operation Bluegill Triple Prime, which finally succeeded on October 25, 1965. However, the brightness of the bomb was unanticipated and multiple military personnel went blind. One military personnel claimed his vision went from 20/25 to 20/400, rendering him legally blind.

However, he would recover after a few months. However, his teammate, who had suffered the same fate, stated that his vision never improved beyond 20/60. On November 1, 1962, the last nuclear bomb under Fishbowl was launched, which detonated over Johnston Atoll.

Today, many consider these tests as evidence of unchecked governmental powers, as they did not think of the effects of the explosions on both the environment and the civilian population.

Operation Northwoods

Operation Northwoods was a planned 1962 terrorist attack on the United States by the U.S. Department of Defence as a pretext for an invasion of Cuba

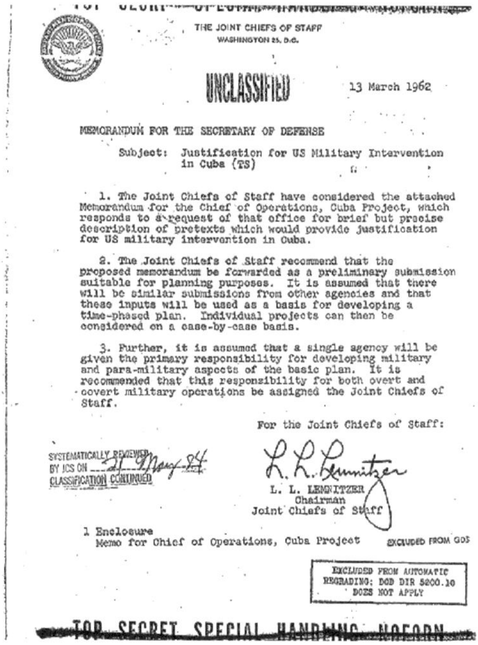

THE JOINT CHIEFS OF STAFF
WASHINGTON 25, D.C.

UNCLASSIFIED

13 March 1962

MEMORANDUM FOR THE SECRETARY OF DEFENSE

Subject: Justification for US Military Intervention in Cuba (TS)

1. The Joint Chiefs of Staff have considered the attached Memorandum for the Chief of Operations, Cuba Project, which responds to a request of that office for brief but precise description of pretexts which would provide justification for US military intervention in Cuba.

2. The Joint Chiefs of Staff recommend that the proposed memorandum be forwarded as a preliminary submission suitable for planning purposes. It is assumed that there will be similar submissions from other agencies and that these inputs will be used as a basis for developing a time-phased plan. Individual projects can then be considered on a case-by-case basis.

3. Further, it is assumed that a single agency will be given the primary responsibility for developing military and para-military aspects of the basic plan. It is recommended that this responsibility for both overt and covert military operations be assigned the Joint Chiefs of Staff.

For the Joint Chiefs of Staff:

SYSTEMATICALLY REVIEWED BY JCS ON 21 May 84 CLASSIFICATION CONTINUED

L. L. Lemnitzer

L. L. LEMNITZER
Chairman
Joint Chiefs of Staff

1 Enclosure
Memo for Chief of Operations, Cuba Project

EXCLUDED FROM GDS

EXCLUDED FROM AUTOMATIC REGRADING; DOD DIR 5200.10 DOES NOT APPLY

~~TOP SECRET SPECIAL HANDLING NOFORN~~

Operation Northwoods document (1962)

Operation Northwoods

In 1962, General Lyman Lemnitzer, Chairman of the Joint Chiefs of Staff, approved a project called Operation Northwoods. It proposed an American invasion of Cuba to end the rule of Fidel Castro by hosting a slew of false flag attacks on the United States and using it as a pretext for the invasion. The operation suggested that the U.S. would hire a Cuban terrorist and make him perpetrate terrorist attacks in Miami, followed by attacks in Washington. Then, there could be a fake passenger plane shot down by Cuba or a staged attack on Guantanamo Bay by soldiers disguised as Cuban soldiers.

Other proposition would be to sabotage the ship of John Glenn, an American astronaut, and let it crash to the ground, killing him instantly. Afterwards, the U.S. could blame the accident on Cuba. Additionally, it proposed to fly a CIA plane over the United States and blow it up to blame it as a false flag pretext to invade Cuba. On March 13, 1962, the operation was finally approved and would find its way to the desk of John F. Kennedy, President of the United States, for final approval, but it would be refused. The project soon found itself in a classified folder, never to be opened again. However, on November 22, 1963, John F. Kennedy was shot and killed by U.S. Marine veteran Lee Harvey Oswald. With him, left a legacy on secrecy of which millions of documents remain classified.

It all changed in 1992, when the U.S. passed the JFK Assassination Records Act, over 4 million documents from his time were declassified. However, because of the whole slew of documents, no one has bothered to read all of them. In 1999, a researcher by the name of Mark J. White published his book "*The Kennedy's and Cuba: The Declassified Documents History*" which brought the document to surface.

It would cause a wide amount of scandal in the United States, leading to widespread conspiracy theories in 2001 that the September 11 attacks were also a false flag operation to invade Afghanistan over natural resources.

COINTELPRO

COINTELPRO was an FBI project between 1956 and 1971, which opted to retaliate against activist groups in the United States.

Fred Hampton after killed by police

An anti-black FBI sting

In a small residential complex in Chicago lived a certain Fred Hampton, whose family struggled financially to make ends meet. Little did they know, Fred would soon become the leader of the Black Panthers, a Black nationalist group tasked with ending police brutality in the streets of Chicago. He was a natural-born speaker and united the streets of Chicago. In 1969, he managed to unite street gangs under the same banner and continued fighting against police brutality. His ability to unify soon became a threat to the FBI, and he entered their watchlist. They sent William O'Neal, a convicted felon, to try to rise among the ranks of the Black Panthers in exchange for his liberty. He soon became Fred Hampton's bodyguard.

On a November night in 1969, William O'Neal slipped several doses of sleeping pills into Fred's drinks, sending him into a comatose state. At 3 a.m., the Chicago PD raided his apartment and shot him three times while he was sleeping. The armed raid was ordered by the FBI themselves. The FBI not only assassinated Black leaders as part of COINTELPRO, they also wiretapped, collected information, and followed them back home. Moreover, the FBI attached itself to local movements like the Mexican-American Chicana/o movements. Members were often instructed to keep their phones in freezers to prevent FBI surveillance.

Puerto Rican revolutionaries were also targeted by the FBI, with their printing presses bombed and their radio broadcasts ended by the FBI. The FBI also targeted the KKK to a lesser extent through surveillance and division.

On March 8, 1971, the Citizen Commission to Investigate the FBI, an activist group, raided the FBI headquarters and uncovered COINTELPRO documents, revealing them to the public. This revelation created massive shock and controversy, forcing the FBI to terminate the program once and for all.

Operation Denver

In the military high-table of the Stasi, a plan for Operation Denver was drafted. It was planned to commence in 1983.

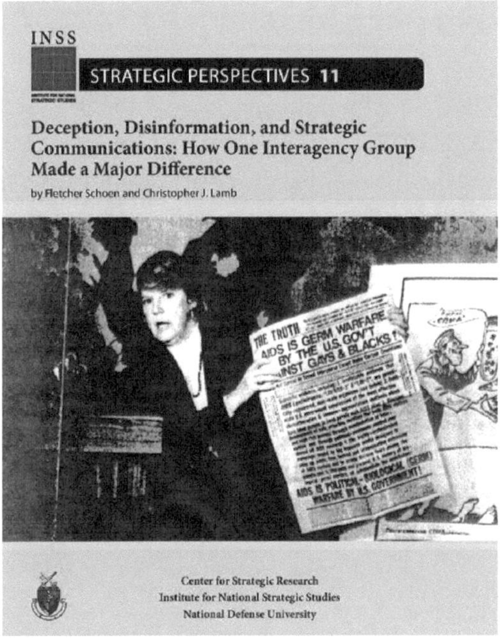

Article on Operation Denver

Modus Operandi

In 1983, in his small office residence in East Berlin, Dr. Jakob Segal, a retired biology professor, received a letter from the East German police. It indicated that they had received proof that the recent AIDS pandemic was a man-made weapon by the United States and not a virus that emerged in Sub-Saharan Africa. The evidence stemmed from a document originating from Fort Detrick, a U.S. biological weapons facility. It stated that they had accidentally spread the flu in San Francisco in 1955, conducted an experiment in Tampa Bay resulting in the death of 12 people, collaborated with the CIA on the Tuskegee Study involving

African Americans, and inadvertently spread HIV. Upon hearing this news, Dr. Jakob Segal was determined to leave retirement and commit himself to spreading this message to the world. He began by holding a conference in Harare, Zimbabwe, where they presented the fact that AIDS started in 1979, three years earlier than its appearance in Africa. In 1986, a brochure titled

> *"AIDS: U.S.A homemade evil, NOT imported from Africa" began spreading across Africa, authored by Prof. J. Segal and Dr. L. Segal.*

Stefan Heym also aided in spreading the message through West Berlin newspapers, reaching the West. In 1987, the KGB contacted the Bulgarian state services to collaborate in spreading this information. In the U.S., the news spread like wildfire, adding legitimacy to existing conspiracy theories surrounding a U.S.-made virus.

In the 1990s, Gorbachev, in an effort to improve relations with the West, ended the disinformation campaign and revealed that it was all a ploy by the KGB. The officials of this operation were finally released from their pact of secrecy and released the book "Auftrag Irreführung: Wie die Stasi Politik im Westen machte" (Mission Deception: How the Stasi Shaped Politics in the West). However, even after the collapse of the Soviet Union in 1991, the conspiracy of a U.S.-made HIV continued to circulate, this time on the internet.

In 2018, an article written by Jakob Segal was spread by *Sputnik News*. Today, this conspiracy still circulates on obscure and fringe websites.

The Holodomor

Between 1932 and 1933, the U.S.SR induced a man-made famine that killed from 2 to 4.5 million people. This genocide was called *The Holodomor*.

Peasants starved to death in Kyiv

Famine and death

In 1933, in Ukraine, Soviet soldiers entered a small village near Kyiv. The village leader was arrested and shot by soldiers. Then, they arrested all leading class members such as religious leaders or teachers. They were told that they had to work collectively on a single farm and that they would come back to collect their dues. The village became silent, and eerie feelings of pain could be felt. The familiar sounds of the old village were gone. In that year, thousands of children from Kyiv entered the countryside begging for food as they were starving. One mother, Mykola Petrenko, remembers burying her two children who had died from famine in the same spot she had buried her relatives a month earlier. Survivors also recall the streets of Kyiv filling with bodies with no one to bury them. The eerie sound of silence prevailed as starving men and women walked over bodies. For survivors, there seemed to be no end to this nightmare.

However, some people experienced a different reality. Some ultra-rich individuals recall leaving for vacation and having plenty of food to eat, while others remember lots of singing in the countryside to try and forget the horrors of the famine. Some survivors recall being laborers or service workers but did not starve as they received a small portion of food from the state, which was sufficient for them to survive. Some survivors also remember hiding food from officials in order to survive. By 1933, over 2-4.5 million people had starved to death.

For the longest time, the Ukrainian famine faded from the collective memories of the world. In 1946, writing competitions were instituted for writers to recount their memories of the famine, but it still remained largely unknown to the rest of the world. It was not until 1986, with the U.S. Commission on Ukrainian Famine, which compelled multiple testimonies of the famine, that news of the horrors of the Holodomor started to spread. Today, the famine is well known in the West and is often the subject of "Holodomor deniers" who deny the existence of the famine despite extensive evidence surrounding it.

Brothers' Home

The Brothers' Home was an internment camp that operated from 1970 to 1980 with the goal of "cleansing" the population of South Korea.

Decade of hell

In 1984, Han, an eight-year-old child, was abducted by a van after his father had left him at a local police station to get groceries. This was the reality of the Brothers' Home Detention Center (형제복지원), a detention center started by the 5th Republic of Korea, considered one of the most brutal dictatorships in Korea's history. In the streets of Korea, "Vagrant Transport" vehicles would wander and search for orphaned children, poor people, the homeless, and those who appeared to be impoverished to seize and transport them in their vans. They would be taken to a remote location in Busan, where they would be given striped, light-blue uniforms.

Each inmate was assigned a number on the back of their clothing. Inmates were then directed by prison officers to their assigned tables where they were forced to manufacture clothing. They were given strict quotas, and if they did not comply, a battalion of other inmates would systematically beat and sometimes kill them. In one case, an inmate who had missed the quota by a few points was dragged out of the factory by a battalion, severely beaten with metal sticks, and left in a pool of blood. Witnessing these beatings left the other inmates terrified and motivated them to work harder to meet the quotas. Every worker inside the factory was paid $10 per month and was not permitted to see family or friends. Among those inside, only 10% were homeless people; the rest had families, and some even had children.

Sights of these beatings had left the other inmates scared and made them work harder in order to fulfill the quotas. Every worker inside the factory was paid $10 every month and were not permitted to see family or friends. From everyone inside, only 10% were homeless.

Many of the abducted children also had parents and were forced to work inside factories while their parents were still searching for them. Many of them were also sold for profit in 'foreign adoption' programs. From 1970 to 1980, over 20,000 children were sold this way. In some cases, the children faced severe abuse in their adoptive families, like Kim Yu-Ri, who was sold to a French family and was systematically abused by her adoptive father. In 2022, the Korean Truth and Reconciliation Commission began investigating the matter. It is still uncovering and investigating the true extent of the camps.

Security Prison 21

Security Prison 21 (S-21) was a torture center for the Khmer Rouge between 1975 to 1979. Over there, they tortured over 20 000 Cambodians with only seven adults surviving.

Tuol Svay Prey high school gym converted into torture cell

A regime of fear

In 1975, troops of the Khmer Rouge staged a coup in Phnom Penh. After they took over the government, they began ordering civilians to leave the big cities and directing them to labor camps in the countryside. Inside, they initiated a new regime based on a socialist agrarian utopia. As part of their policies, they started a series of purges targeting individuals they suspected to be against the regime. These included people who worked for the old government, those suspected to have connections with foreign governments, Buddhist monks, as well as individuals who "looked intelligent" (such as people with glasses or those who spoke multiple languages). These definitions were often very vague, and anyone could become a target of the purge. Once selected, these people would be sent to the notorious Security Prison S-21 also known as the Hill of the Poisonous Trees.

It was an old high school situated in Phnom Penh, the capital of Cambodia. Upon arrival, prisoners would be photographed, interviewed, and then led to their shed to be shackled to a metal bar. During the day, they had no clothes, were forced to eat a mediocre bland of watery rice and were subject to torture including waterboarding, suffocation with plastic bags, nail removal, operations without anesthesia, forced consumption of human feces, and more. Most inmates would eventually confess to the made-up crimes and even agree to record it in front of a camera. Afterwards, they would endure further torture for two to three months before eventually being executed.

Many foreigners were also captured and executed in these camps as well. This was the case of Americans James Clark and Lance McNamara who went on a sailing trip in Southeast Asia. They had planned to land in Thailand, but their boat had drifted off-course, and they ended up in Cambodia. They were taken by Khmer Rouge soldiers and sent to S-21 where they were ruthlessly tortured. They were forced to confess that they were working for the CIA and had observed that Cambodia was the most successful communist country in the world. Two months later, they were both executed.

The terror of Khmer Rouge would eventually end in 1979 after Vietnamese forces would arrive in Phnom Penh.

Operation Sea-Spray

Operation Sea-Spray was a biological attack by the U.S. Navy on San Francisco as part of an experiment by the United States Army.

USS De-Long (1943)

The Experiment Unfolds

On a foggy morning in September 1950, Navy vessels stationed near the Golden Gate Bridge began spraying a blend of *Serratia marcescens* and an inert chemical tracer into the air. The aim was to simulate a biological attack and track how these microorganisms would disperse across the densely populated area. For six days, the bacteria were released into the atmosphere, carried by the winds, and spread across the city. The Navy monitored the spread of the bacteria by placing sampling devices at 43 locations throughout San Francisco. The results indicated that the bacteria had disseminated widely, with nearly all residents exposed to the microorganism within a matter of days.

At the time, *Serratia marcescens* was considered harmless, but this assumption proved dangerously incorrect. Following the experiment, there was a spike in rare urinary tract infections at Stanford University's hospital, and a patient named Edward J. Nevin died from a heart valve infection caused by Serratia marcescens. This incident raised serious questions about the safety and ethics of the operation. Many residents were unaware of the experiment and its potential health risks. The secrecy surrounding Operation Sea-Spray only intensified public fear and mistrust when the details eventually came to light. In subsequent years, it became evident that the experiment had violated ethical principles and posed significant health risks to the unsuspecting population.

The operation was part of a broader program of biological warfare testing conducted by the U.S. military during the Cold War. These tests were designed to understand the vulnerability of American cities to biological attacks and to develop strategies for defense. However, the methods employed often ignored the potential harm to civilians. In the years following Operation Sea Spray, revelations about similar experiments conducted across the United States emerged, leading to public outcry and calls for greater transparency and accountability in military research.

The legacy of Operation Sea Spray remains a stark reminder of the ethical dilemmas and potential dangers of using civilians as unwitting test subjects in military experiments.

CIA Drug Trafficking

CIA drug trafficking is an allegation against the Central Intelligence Agency, accusing it of being involved in drug trafficking activities since 1947.

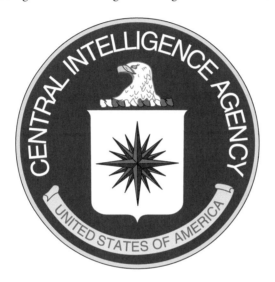

Drug Empire

The first allegations of CIA drug trafficking began in 1949 in a drug-hotspot called the *Golden Triangle*. Within it, it is suspected that the CIA trafficked drugs within the Golden Triangle, a drug-hotspot in Southeast Asia and smuggled drugs to Laos in order to fund their war against communist insurgents called the *Pathet Lao*. In order to do so, the CIA also operated a covert airline called Air America, a civilian aircraft fleet that transported weapons, U.S. personnel, wounded soldiers, commando units, refugees and allegedly, also drugs. As well, the CIA also allegedly worked the Corsican gangs to produce heroin to be distributed to France. It was led by Corsican gang leader, Paul Carbone, who, between 1937-1967, was protected by the CIA to distribute heroin in exchange of preventing the Old Port of Marseilles to be taken over by the French Communists.

In Latin America, the CIA allegedly aided terrorist and rebel leaders within the Contras movement (see "Contras") to sell and distribute cocaine and other drugs in Latin America. These drugs would all be eventually smuggled into major American cities like Los Angeles fueling the drug pandemic. These drugs would also fuel dangerous drug wars in Latin America which still persists to this day. In October 2013, it was also suspected that the CIA had assassinated secret DEA operative Kiki Camarena, because he was a threat to the CIA's drug trafficking in Mexico in the 1980s.

However, it was subsequently denied by a CIA spokesperson.

In 2009, rumors had spread that the CIA was funding drug trafficking in Afghanistan where the brother of the president, Ahmed Wali Karzai, was reportedly receiving regular payments from the CIA in order to traffic heroin in Afghanistan. This too has vehemently been denied by the CIA. To conclude, through multiple occasions, the CIA had been seen to be open to drug trafficking (if these allegations are true) despite having a very anti-drug and pro-citizen view on the outside.

Clandestine Radios

Wardenclyffe Tower (1904)

- *La Voz de la Liberación (100.5 FM) was a radio station established by the CIA with the aim of destabilizing Guatemala. It frequently labeled the president, Jacobo Arbenz, as a communist and encouraged the public to overthrow the government.*
- *Radio Swan (1165 AM) was a clandestine radio station created by the CIA to disseminate anti-Fidel Castro propaganda from Swan Island located near the coast of Honduras.*

A nine-second excerpt is currently available on YouTube under the title "Emisora radial contra Cuba: Radio Swan."

- *Radio Hanoi (90 FM) was a propaganda news channel established by North Vietnam to mock American soldiers. Its most famous broadcast featured "Hanoi*

Hannah," who would taunt American soldiers by mentioning specific details such as the names of their ships.

You can now find this broadcast under the title "Hanoi Hannah–The world-famous GI JOE broadcaster" on YouTube.

- *Radio Télévision des Milles Collines (RTLM) was a radio station launched in 1993 that initially played popular music and gained popularity among the populace. However, it gradually transformed into a platform for spreading hate, adding inflammatory content to its broadcasts. In 1994, it incited hatred against the Tutsi people, contributing significantly to the onset of the Rwandan genocide.*

You can listen to excerpts from its broadcasts during the genocide in 1994 by searching for "Excerpts from RTLM broadcasts during the genocide in 1994."

- *Radio Venceremos (104.9 FM): An underground anti-government radio set up by the rebels during the Salvadoran Civil War.*

You can listen to it freely by searching "Radio Venceremos" on YouTube!

- *Radio Free Derry (240 AM): During the Troubles period of Ireland, Irish nationalist set up anti-British radios that broadcast rebel songs and encouraging resistance against the British forces.*

You can listen to it by searching "Radio Free Derry (The Troubles, Northern Ireland 1969)" on YouTube.

Pinkerton Agency

The Pinkerton Agency was a private detective agency founded by Scottish-American Allan Pinkerton and Chicago attorney Edward Rucker. They gained notoriety for their ruthless tactics employed against union workers, criminals, and perceived enemies of the state.

Pinkerton's slogan, "We Never Sleep"

"We never sleep"

The Pinkerton Agency was a private security agency often hired by the government or railroad companies to provide surveillance or protection services. It was created in the 1850s and was originally hired by railroad companies to prevent robberies and sabotage. However, by 1860, tensions were growing between the North and the South, leading to the American Civil War. This conflict provided more business opportunities for Pinkerton. One notable case is the Baltimore plot in 1861, where the Pinkerton agency discovered a plot involving several pro-Confederate paramilitaries and secret groups planning to sabotage railways and assassinate Lincoln. By warning Lincoln of the plot, Pinkerton assigned their top agent, Kate Warne, who devised several elaborate schemes to thwart the plans of the assassins throughout the night, allegedly saving the president's life. During the mission, she did not sleep, leading to Pinkerton's slogan: *"We never sleep."*

During this time, Pinkerton also deployed a series of agents in the South who acted as spies gathering intelligence. However, their intelligence was often incorrect and exaggerated, leading to the loss of contracts with Lincoln. Nevertheless, Pinkerton's operations continued into the 1870s and 1880s, during which they were tasked with capturing the top criminals and bandits of the Wild West.

In it, they quickly became known for their violence and their quick use of it. For example, in 1875, to capture members of the James Gang, the Pinkerton agency threw an incendiary device on their home, burning the right arm of James's wife and killing their 9-year-old son. In 1877, they were hired by the U.S. government to end the Railway Strike of 1877 and engaged in violent labor suppression, which resulted in approximately 10-13 deaths. They also worked for American industrialist Andrew Carnegie and engaged in beating union strikes within his steel factories. Today, the Pinkerton Agency still exists and has been known to have been hired by large mega-corporations like Amazon or Starbucks to install corporate spies within the workforce to surveil for any signs of unionization or discussions of unions between workers.

Operation PX

Operation PX, also known as Operation Cherry Blossoms at Night, was a planned biological weapon attack by Imperial Japan on Los Angeles, San Diego, and numerous other cities on the West Coast of the United States during World War II.

Japanese attack on Pearl Harbor

A biological attack

During WWII, Japan felt threatened by the United States for concealing its position as the leading power in Asia. It believed war against the United States was inevitable. To deter American interventionism, it initiated its attack on Pearl Harbor in Hawaii to weaken the United States in a preemptive strike. However, the attack backfired, and the United States retaliated against Japan. By then, Japan had begun attacks on the mainland of the United States, notably with the bombing of Ellwood in Santa Barbara or the deployment of Fu-Go bombs on the continental United States. In 1945, Japan began a new plan, Operation PX or Operation Cherry Blossoms at Night, an aerial attack on the United States that would launch bombs charged with weaponized bubonic plague, cholera, or dengue fever, which would spread across the United States.

However, some officials at the decision board disagreed with the plan. Notably, Yoshijirō Umezu, a senior general, showed strong opposition to the project, explaining that *"If bacterial warfare is conducted, it will not become a war between Japan and the United States, but a war between bacteria and the world."* After his strong opposition, the plan was cancelled, and Japan continued its fight against the United States. Five months later, two nuclear bombs were dropped on two of its major cities, Hiroshima and Nagasaki. It surrendered shortly afterward.

On September 2, 1945, Japan formally surrendered to the United States. One of the senior proponents of the plan, Shiro Ishii, was distraught by the surrender and contemplated carrying out the plan himself. He envisioned charging into Los Angeles with a plane filled with bubonic plague and dying in a suicide attack.

However, his superiors rejected this idea and instructed him to remain patient, waiting for a more opportune moment instead of acting rashly. Shortly after that, the United States contacted Ishii. In exchange for his research on bacterial warfare, he was offered immunity for war crimes, particularly his involvement in torture camps during his tenure as Unit 731 head. After providing his research, Ishii was indeed granted immunity and never faced any punishment for his actions.

Black Cube

Black Cube is a private intelligence agency founded by ex-members of the Mossad in 2010, they have been associated with a wide-amount of controversies

Black Cube logo

The Oligarch's Archangel

In 2010, Avi Yanus, a member of the Israeli Defence Forces (IDF) founded Black Cube alongside another intelligence officer. In its reign, it has been involved in gathering intelligence in over 80 different countries of which many claim were gathered in covert and illegal ways. One of its most controversial clients was Hollywood oligarch and director, Harvey Weinstein who is now accused on multiple counts of sexual assault. In 2016, Harvey contracted Black Cube to help him against his sexual assault allegations of which Black Cube hired multiple female agents posing as human rights activities to attempt to extract information for Harvey's victims in order to discredit them.

Another controversial client was Donald Trump, an American businessman and President of the United States between 2017-2021. In 2017, he hired Black Cube in order to "dig up dirt" on the Iran Nuclear deal in order to undermine the Obama administration which ultimately failed. Another powerful politician that hired

Black Cube was Joseph Kabila, president of the Democratic Republic of Congo (DRC) who under Operation Coltan in 2015, hired Black Cube to spy on his political opponents which attracted a wide amount of controversy internationally when it was revealed. As well, Black Cube does not only serve powerful politicians and rich oligarchs but also wealthy mega-corporations.

In 2015, Black Cube helped Taiwanese shipping company TMT win a $47 M lawsuit of which it got the case dismissed when it discovered a missing claiming which resulted in the dismissal of the case. In 2016, it also helped Rami Levy Chain Stores, a massive supermarket chain store in Israel expose a negative press campaign by their competitors by providing evidence on the PR manager who had tried to damage Rami Levy's reputation. In 2019, it helped protect a powerful Israeli spyware company called NSO Group by trying to portray two University of Toronto cyber security researchers as antisemitic by goading them using undercover agents.

Nevertheless, Black Cube has left a legacy of fear and questioning on the privatization of intelligence which has become a multi-million-dollar industry where companies "pay for spying" in order to win million-dollar lawsuits questioning the equality of our current justice system for the less-economically privileged.

Abu Ghraib Prison Scandal

The Abu Ghraib was a prison operated by the United States government in which its soldiers tortured and toyed with soldiers for the sake of fun.

"The Hooded Man"

The prison

In 2004, Seymour Hersh, a reporter was sent a series of pictures by an anonymous source. It showed prisoners who were stripped naked by soldiers and forced to be bit by dogs, being forced to build human pyramids, being electrocuted or being brutally beat for fun. Traumatized, he inquired about the location of the prison and the source revealed it was the Abu Ghraib prison in Iraq which was operated by the United States at that time. He had previously seen and published pictures of the My Lai Massacre in Vietnam and knew how important it would be to release these documents. These documents weren't just released to Seymour but to multiple news outlets. In April 2004, a report titled *60 Minutes* aired on CBC News detailing the brutality and inhumanity inside American prisons in Iraq. Subsequently, Seymour Hersh would publish his article showing all the pictures he had received from the scandal. When these pictures released, the American public was shocked. Even though news of these abuses had been widely available to the public prior to the 2004 releases.

Nevertheless, in Seymour's 2004 release, the picture that had captivated the public the most was the picture of "The Hooded Man". It was a picture of a man who was forced to wear a hood and forced stand on a box and has multiple wires attached to his fingers. From what we understand, the prisoner would receive an electric shock whenever he moved, and he was forced to stand there for hours.

Other pictures included a U.S. soldier holding a bound Iraqi prisoner in a headlock while senselessly punching him in the head. Another picture features a soldier posing and smiling in front of the deceased and decomposed corpse of a tortured Iraqi prisoner. Many of these pictures can still be found by searching "Abu Ghraib Prison Picture" on Google (TW: these pictures are extremely unsettling).

When these pictures were revealed, the U.S. government attempted to suppress them, deeming the pictures unpatriotic and a threat to U.S. troops. However, their efforts to halt the release of these images proved unsuccessful. These shocking pictures left a permanent mark on the reputation of the United States, forever associating the nation with the heinous acts of torture and abuse.

Chapter II:
Ominous

The next pages may contain some **shocking content** (either hidden in the embed links or in the general picture). Please read with caution. The same **warning** applies to this chapter.

Lavender Town Syndrome

The Lavender Town Syndrome is an urban legend that suggests Japanese children in the 1990s committed suicide after entering the level due to the eerie atmosphere and music.

Lavender Town reproduction

Pokemon cemetery

In 1996, Nintendo released Pokémon Red and Blue for the Game Boy. The game featured a young boy named Red, who starts his journey in the small town of Pallet Town. Players could choose between three starter Pokémon: Bulbasaur, Charmander, and Squirtle, before setting out to catch more Pokémon. Along the way, players could explore different regions to catch various types of Pokémon, challenge Pokémon gyms to earn badges, and ultimately become Pokémon champions. After visiting Viridian City, Pewter City, and Saffron City, players eventually arrived at Route 8, which leads them to Lavender Town.

Upon entering the town, players would hear eerie music and come face-to-face with the Pokémon Tower, an eight-level tower functioning as a cemetery. Inside, multiple Pokémon trainers would stand mourning their deceased Pokémon, while numerous ghost Pokémon roamed the area, allowing players to capture them. In 2010, an urban legend emerged alleging that Pokémon players in the 1990s, many of them children, had killed themselves due to the eerie music of Lavender Town.

This legend gained widespread attention, and additional information began to surface. Some posters purported that the Pokémon Unown formed the phrase *"Leave now"*, adding to the ominous atmosphere of the level.

Upon further investigation, it was discovered that the Lavender Town Syndrome story first emerged on a website called *Creepypasta*. This site is known for hosting convincing horror stories that have fooled numerous people. One of its most popular stories is "The Russian Sleep Experiment," which speculates about Russians testing the effects of severe sleep deprivation on their soldiers using a gas that kept them awake for days, resulting in them becoming violent, zombie-like creatures.

Today, both the Lavender Town Syndrome and "The Russian Sleep Experiment" are widely regarded as urban legends, illustrating the power of storytelling and the internet to create and spread myths and folklore.

Nazi Gold Train

The Nazi Gold Train is an urban legend about a train filled with stolen gold and paintings in Europe, supposedly hidden inside the *Riese* underground complex in Poland.

Nazi Gold Train alleged location

Riese Complex

In September 1943, as Germany's defeat seemed inevitable, the Minister of War, Albert Speer, spearheaded "Der Riese" or "The Giant," a system of underground tunnels and factories intended to sustain the Nazis' grip on power. The complex was designed to shield the Nazis from the increasing Allied bombings and allow them to continue weapon production to fight against the advancing Allies. Beginning in 1943, over 13,000 individuals, predominantly from the Soviet Union and Poland, were forced to build the tunnels. Death became commonplace as malnourished workers collapsed on the floor, their bodies stacking up as construction progressed.

When progress slowed, Adolf Hitler ordered the integration of workers from concentration camps, primarily Jews, into the workforce. Conditions remained perilous, with outbreaks of typhus and limited progress. By 1945, as the tanks of the Soviet Red Army approached, the Nazis abandoned the project, leaving behind a scene of devastation. Upon arrival, the Soviets discovered a mass of corpses, the majority succumbing to malnutrition, illness, or abuse. It was revealed that these individuals had been working on a tunnel complex intended to house various factories for weapon manufacturing. However, the project was never completed, and no factories were operational inside the tunnel. Nonetheless, a widespread urban legend persists surrounding the tunnel.

Allegedly, towards the end of World War II, the Nazis purportedly drove an armored train into the tunnel filled with stolen goods from Europe, including gold, paintings, and necklaces, hoping to conceal it from the Allies. In 2015, two Polish men claimed to have discovered the tunnel using radar technology. The Polish military was mobilized to search for the train, but no evidence of its existence was found. Today, the area has become a popular tourist destination, with a fictional "Nazi Gold Train" attraction. However, it is crucial not to overlook the atrocities committed by the Nazis to construct this tunnel and the human toll it exacted during its construction.

HINTERKAIFECK Murders

The Hinterkaifeck Murders were a series of unsolved murders in a farm in Bavaria in 1922.

HINTERKAIFECK farm location

Murders in the Orient

On April 4, 1922, a local farmer in the area, Lorenz Schlittenbauer, went in the Gruber family's house to investigate as they had not left their house for multiple days. They were all found dead. Six months prior to the attack, the family maid left because she had heard strange sounds around the farm despite being alone. She felt uneasy and felt the farm was haunted which led her to quit. During that time, the patriarch of the family, Andreas Gruber experienced strange incidents during that time. Once, he had received a copy of the *Munich Newspaper*, but he had never subscribed to it. Another time, he had left one of his house keys on the table, but it suddenly disappeared making him doubt whether he misplaced them. The last time, he had heard someone in the attic even though none of his family were in it.

On March 31, 1922, the new maid, Maria Baumgartner, arrived alongside her sister at the farm. Her sister would accompany her, but eventually leave her to the farm, she would be the last one that would ever see the family again. On that day, Maria would claim to have seen footsteps in the snow leading to the barn area, but did not recognize the footprint as it did not belong to anyone in the family. In the next few days, an unknown killer would lure members of the family individually by rattling the barn and killing them with a mattock (half axe/ half hoe) to the head.

Following the murder of all five family members (including the maid), the killer moved to the kitchen area and ate the family's food for a few days before leaving into the woods, never to be seen again. After the murder, it was reported that a strange man had been roaming in the vicinity asking about crime until he ran into the forest after proclaiming he was the killer.

However, the strange man was never caught. Other suspects of the murder was Karl Gabriel, a family members' (Viktoria) ex-husband who had died during WW1, but his body was never found. Some suspected he came back after the war, seeking revenge on the family that had abandoned him a long time ago.

Flannan Lighthouse Disappearances

The Flannan Lighthouse Disappearances was a series of disappearances on December 15th of 1900 in the Flannan Isles.

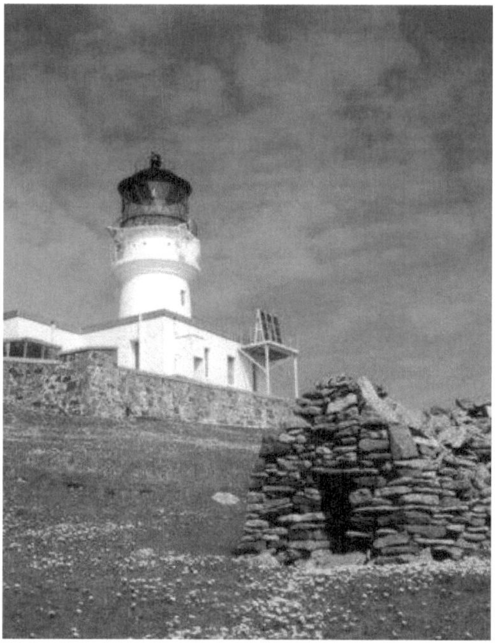

Flannan Isle Lighthouse

Gone with the wind

On December 15th, 1900, a ship, the *Herberus*, docking in the Flannan Isles felt something was off as the lighthouse keepers did not come down and greet them as they usually did. In response, the captain, Joseph Moore, went out and climbed over 160 steps up the lighthouse before discovering it completely empty. The lighthouse was previously manned by three men, James Ducat, Thomas Marshall, and William MacArthur, who on that day, had reset the clock on the wall, and set the table and left a canary in the cage were nowhere to be seen. When he went down, he would find an oilskin (used for protection against the cold weather), a removed railway track and a smashed supply box. In response, the crew of the Herberus spread out in the island for the search of the three men, but had found the island completely empty.

One theory that would explain the disappearance of the three men was the foul play theory. According to some witnesses, William MacArthur, one of the lighthouse keepers, was an ill-tempered man and would often respond to events using violence. Henceforth, one of the speculations is that MacArthur, on that day, would have gotten into a violent argument with his colleagues and would engage in a fist-fight ultimately killing them both. He would then throw both bodies off the cliff and jump off as well out of guilt. Another theory is the storm theory. According to diaries and weather reports, a storm was heading in the area the previous day which made maneuvers difficult.

It is possible that James Ducat and Thomas Marshall had gone out to fix damage to the lighthouse, but were destabilized by the strong winds of the storm and fell to their death. In response, William MacArthur would check on them after some time and would himself fall off the cliff due to the strong winds.

Nevertheless, despite the plausibility of these two theories, none of them have been proven and the bodies of the three lighthouse keepers were never found, leaving the mystery of the Flannan Lighthouse, unsolved.

The Hump

The Hump was an area in the Himalayan mountains notorious for a significant number of disappearances of Allied aircraft during World War II.

"The Hump"

Flying Tigers

In 1942, the Americans sought to support Chiang Kai-Shek's government by flying supplies through the eastern end of the Himalayan mountains to China. This was aimed at resupplying the Chinese Army, which had been pushed back from their capital and was running low on supplies. The task was assigned to the U.S.A.A.F Tenth Air Force and other Allied troops, including the First American Volunteer Group (AVG), famously known as The Flying Tigers. The flights were exceptionally perilous, as pilots relied on the technique known as "Dead Reckoning." According to historian John D. Plating, pilots would navigate by choosing a direction for a specific amount of time before attempting to land. Flying at an altitude of 25 000 feet, pilots essentially flew blind. During the operation, numerous planes crashed in the Himalayas or disappeared entirely. One of the main contributors to these losses was the U.S. Air Force's Flying Tigers, which included over 200 Chinese-Americans, among them the legendary air fighter Albert Mah.

Albert Mah recalled the Hump as being especially treacherous, with planes frequently being shot down or crashing into the mountains. He also remembered that the most perilous moments weren't during flights, but rather the constant threat of Japanese attacks on their camps. On one occasion, he broadcasted the song "*The Sweetest Mile is the Last Mile Home*" with his saxophone over the radio to fellow pilots while his base was under attack by the Japanese.

Because of his song, other pilots who had been enjoying the music couldn't hear the alert message broadcast. When they returned to their base, they discovered that their operating center had been destroyed by fire. Albert Mah faced significant controversy from his colleagues following the incident. Nonetheless, he survived one of the deadliest air operations in history. He passed away peacefully at St. Mary's Hospital in Montreal, Canada, at the age of 84.

Today, it is estimated that over 594 aircraft were lost during the operation, and more than 1659 military personnel disappeared or died on the mission.

Barnum's American Museum

Barnum's American Museum was a museum and freak-show hosted by American businessman, P.T. Barnum between 1841 and 1864.

Barnum's American Museum in 1853

Come on in!

In 1841, P.T. Barnum, an American businessman opened an oddity museum called Barnum's American Museum. At its peak, it received over 15,000 visitors a year. Within the museum, it featured a vast cast of characters like Chang and Eng, Siamese twins, Grizzly Adams' (an American mountaineer) trained bears, a Fiji mermaid (a fake), midgets, giants as well as General Tom Thumb, a 35-inch-tall dwarf. As well, the museum contained dioramas, panoramas of landmarks, scientific instruments, an oyster bar, the tree where Jesus supposedly sat on, and a giant aquarium containing beluga whales.

The museum was an eccentric containment of entertainment which by 1853 had become a problem as the museum had become too crowded due to people staying too long. To counter the problem, P.T. Barnum had placed a sign saying "This Way to the Egress" of which when the visitors followed the sign, they would end up outside (Egress meant outside). As well, P.T. Barnum would get in wide amounts of controversy where many of his exhibits like the Fiji Mermaid was fake, but had only found to make his museum more popular as people wanted to see it themselves. It was shown later that P.T. Barnum would often anonymously write news article calling his museum as "fake" to encourage people to go and see themselves if it was truly fake. The museum became a vast success where it was even visited by Queen Elizabeth.

In 1864, the museum was fire-bombed by eight agents belonging to the Confederate Army of Manhattan which set fire to over 18 buildings in New York including the museum. However, it was quickly extinguished. A couple of months later, in July 1864, the building burned down again, this time for good. Animals that had jumped out of the building were shot by the NYPD and a tiger had been axed by the New York fire department. It was over for the museum.

Barnum would eventually re-open the museum under Barnum's New Museum, but it would never have the same success and also burned down in 1868 ending the idea of the museum forever.

Heaven's Gate

Heaven's gate was a new-age UFO religious movement who committed mass-suicide on March 22-26 of 1997.

Aliens are coming!

On March 22 of 1997, members of Heaven's Gate began preparing a concoction of phenobarbital mixed with applesauce and vodka before wrapping their faces in plastic wraps and committing suicide. The process was done via groups and once a group had killed themselves, the second group would hide the first group face with purple clothes before committing suicide themselves. This was done over the span of four days upon the arrival of Comet Hale–Bopp which they believed was the sign that they could send their body to "the New Level" or Heaven's Gate. According to the leader of Heaven's Gate, Marshall Applewhite (see picture), Jesus Christ of Nazareth, a prophet and messiah in the Christian religion, was possessed by an otherworldly alien which gave him supernatural powers. He would claim that he was possessed by the same alien and came to Earth as another Messiah.

According to him, humanity had to renounce its worldly possessions and transfer itself to a new heavenly body. He also believed that the government would persecute them and that he had to find disciples called "*The Crew*" to join him in the afterlife. During his recruitment, he prayed on vulnerable and lonely people to recruit to his cult before indoctrination them to his ideas, giving them a sense of purpose. In October 1996, he rented out a large house called *the Monastery*, a 9,200-square-foot mansion, of which his followers would live in. On that same month, he would also purchase alien abduction insurance and began preaching to his followers that a UFO would abduct them and bring them to a plane of existence "above humanity".

In order to be abducted, he explained that his followers needed to renounce their physical body through asphyxiation and that the comet who was arriving that year (Hale–Bopp) was followed by an extraterrestrial ship. By performing the ritual, all of his followers would rise up to the ship. On March 26, 1997, San Diego's 911 system received an alarming call:

Sheriff's Department: 911 what's your emergency?

Caller: Yes, I need to report an anonymous tip, who do I talk to?

Sheriff's Department: Okay, this is regarding what?

Caller: This is regarding a mass suicide, and I can give you the address ...

"Sorry my baby"

"Sorry My Baby" is an urban legend associated with the band "Grasshopper, released in 1993. According to the legend, the song was played extensively in the Shanghai Pacific Mall in 2013 to drown out the sounds of crying babies who had died there during the Sino-Japanese War.

Shanghai Pacific Mall today

The Tale of the Haunted Song

"Grasshopper" was a Hong Kong boy band that gained popularity after releasing their first album in 1988. One of their popular songs was called "Sorry My Baby". In 2013, reports from netizens in China claimed to have heard babies crying in the Shanghai Pacific Mall, along with discovering bite marks on toys. Subsequently, it was reported that the mall hired a Feng Shui expert to investigate the situation.

According to the expert's analysis, the mall was built on the site of an old French nursery established in 1920. Tragically, in 1937, the orphanage was bombed by the Japanese Imperial forces, resulting in the deaths of all the orphans inside. When the Shanghai Pacific Mall opened in the 1990s on the same location, it was believed to have housed the spirits of the deceased orphans.

The Feng Shui master recommended playing the song "Sorry My Baby" every day to ward off the hauntings, which explained the consistent playing of the song in 2013. However, this urban legend is surrounded by controversy, with many netizens claiming that there is no evidence to support such claims and suggesting that the mall played the song simply because it was popular at the time.

Today, the store has been closed down and replaced by a new and more modern storefront called the Ruian Plaza. No new hauntings have been reported in the area, and it has become a vibrant part of Shanghai.

The Grasshopper band continues to grow in fame today, with members performing around the world. Additionally, some members of the group have opened their own YouTube channels, such as Remus Choy who opened his channel called Remus Kitchen (傑少煮意) which focuses on his love for cooking as well as the band had created The Grasshopper Channel focusing on the artist's personality and featuring select interview to help the audience bond with the singer even without the song!

You can still listen to *Sorry My Baby* by Grasshopper today by searching "Grass-hopper sorry my baby" on Youtube!

Africanized Bees

Africanized Bees, also known as *Killer Bees*, were a man-made hybrid created in the 1950s by Brazilian geneticist Dr. Warwick E. Kerr. This bee led to hundreds of deaths and economic devastation to the areas it spread.

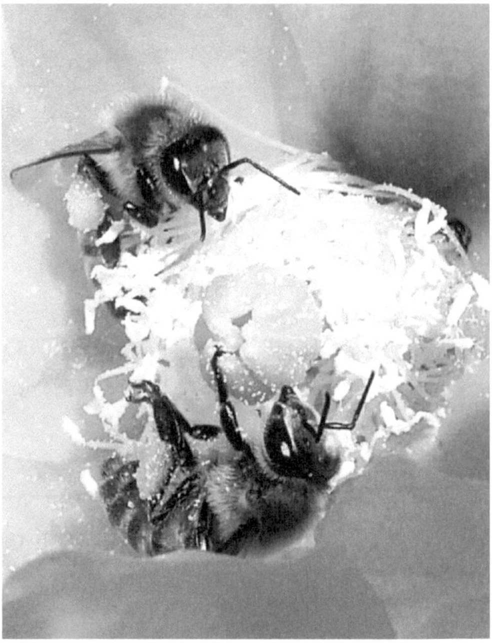

Africanized bees in action

An insect invasion

In 1956, Brazilian geneticist Dr. Warwick E. Kerr aimed to boost honey production in Brazil. His innovative idea involved creating a genetically modified bee by crossbreeding the European bee with the East African bee.

This endeavor sought to combine the desirable traits of the European bee's high honey production with the East African bee's resistance to warm climates. During Kerr's research in 1957, more than 20 colonies of African bees vanished from his lab and interbred with nearby bees, resulting in the emergence of a deadly variant known as the Killer bee or Africanized bee. By 1986, these Africanized bees had spread to Mexico, followed by Texas in 1990 and California in 1994. The East African bees held a significant advantage over European bees due to their increased hostility, stemming from their evolution in Africa alongside more natural predators. These Africanized bees rapidly spread, moving at a rate of 400 km per year and forming swarms containing anywhere from 300,000 to 800,000 individuals.

In Mexico, they expanded their territory to approximately 16 million km^2, wreaking havoc on local colonies through resource extraction, nesting competitiveness, and parasite transmission. To survive, many native bee species were forced to alter their foraging methods to avoid direct competition with Africanized bees.

Numerous native bee species, such as *Perdita meconis* and *Eucera quadricincta*, were driven to extinction by the aggressive invasion of Africanized bees.

However, some positive outputs have been attributed to Africanized bees. Many of the natural honey bees predators like the Army ants now target these new bees that are much more hostile than regular honey bees which allows the honey bees to thrive in their climates.

Nevertheless, even in 2024, Africanized bees are considered a threat to the native species, but have been declining since the 2000s because of the heavy use of insecticide and pesticide in modern agriculture.

Malleus Maleficarum

"Malleus Maleficarum" (or the Witches' Hammer) was a witchcraft treatise that became the staple book of witch-hunters from the 14th to the 15th century.

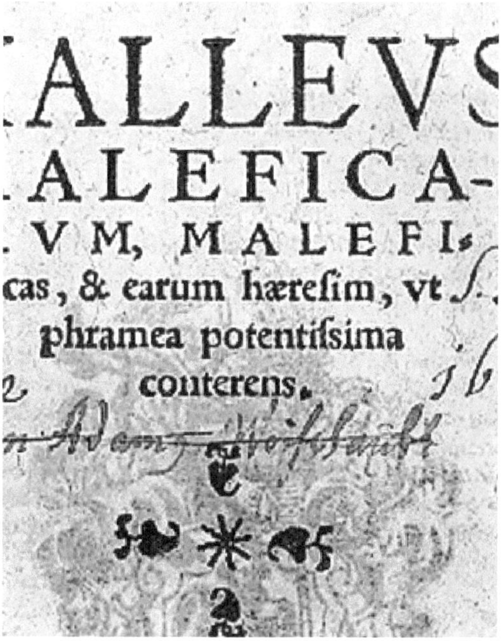
ALLEVS
ALEFICA-
VM, MALEFI-
cas, & earum hæresim, vt
phramea potentissima
conterens.

Malleus Maleficarum's cover

A book that invites violence

Many scholars have labeled it the most evil book after Hitler's *Mein Kampf*, while others have deemed it the most cruel and misogynistic book in the history of mankind. However, for Heinrich Kramer, a member of the Inquisition who advocated for the hunting of witches, it was his bible. In 1486, Kramer began pushing for the persecution of witches as a form of heresy, which was a crime at the time. He recommended illegal techniques such as torturing women to extract confessions and burning them alive as punishment.

In his treatise, the Malleus Maleficarum, Kramer predominantly defined witches as female, attributing their alleged carnal lust to their insatiable pursuit of witchcraft. He employed a variety of "proof" to convince skeptics of the criminality and existence of witchcraft, including anecdotal evidence from his experiences as an Inquisitor and references to past works like Isidore's *Etymologiae*, which described witches practicing harmful magic. Kramer also propagated the belief that witches could magically rob young men of their private parts, a notion derived from old folklore.

Additionally, he outlined the judicial process for handling witch trials, advocating for torture to extract confessions and burning at the stake as punishment. With the advent of the Gutenberg printing press in the late 15th century, Kramer's message spread rapidly, fueling a witch hysteria in which women were hunted, tortured, and burned at the stake with little to no evidence.

This period gave rise to widespread misogynistic violence, as tortured witches would often provide names of others, leading to further witch hunts. In total, it is estimated that between 35,000 to 50,000 women were executed for witchcraft between 1450 and 1750.

However, it would be inaccurate to attribute the sole cause of witchcraft to the *Malleus Maleficarum*. Other factors contributed to the phenomenon, including the growing influence of the Catholic Church. The papal bull issued by Pope Innocent VIII, which authorized the hunting of witches, fueled the growing paranoia surrounding witchcraft.

Battle of Los Angeles

The Battle of Los Angeles was an incident that occurred during World War II, where the 37th U.S. Artillery Coast Guard Brigade engaged in a conflict with what was believed to be a Japanese air force.

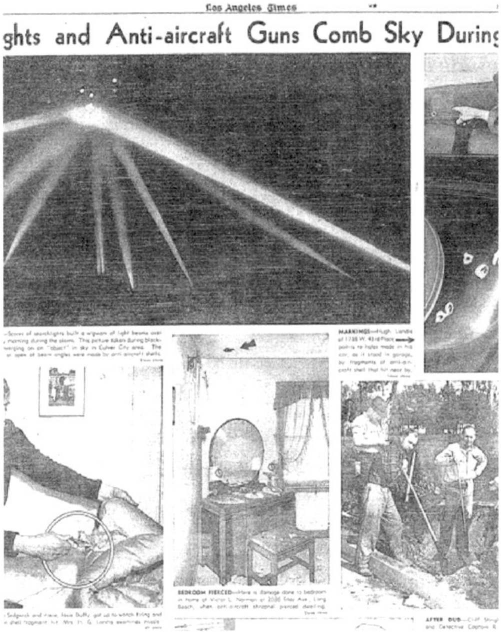
Los Angeles Times

ghts and Anti-aircraft Guns Comb Sky Durin

Battle of Los Angeles featured in the LA Times in 1942

Alarms activated

On February 23, 1942, California experienced a bombardment by a Japanese submarine off the coast of Ellwood. This event sparked widespread fear across the West Coast, leaving citizens on edge. The following day, February 24, 1942, at 2:26 a.m., air sirens sounded in Los Angeles, signaling an imminent Japanese attack. A citywide blackout was enforced, with citizens instructed to use dark curtains to conceal any light, and all public lighting was extinguished to prevent Japanese aircraft from identifying the city. The blackout led to multiple car accidents, resulting in at least three deaths and two heart attacks. Within minutes of the blackout, troops from Santa Monica mobilized their anti-aircraft guns and commenced firing into the sky in an effort to intercept enemy aircraft. News reports announced that Los Angeles was under attack by swarms of enemy planes, with claims of multiple downed aircraft in West Hollywood. Powerful searchlights were deployed to scan the sky for enemy pilots. Meanwhile, the 37th U.S. Artillery Coast Guard Brigade continued firing into the sky, creating a cloud of smoke. By 4:14 a.m., the sky had cleared, and the military launched an investigation after expending over 1,400 rounds of anti-aircraft ammunition. Despite citizen reports of aircraft sightings, no enemy or downed aircraft were found.

However, some individuals, like Charles Patrick, a member of the U.S. artillery guard, claimed to have engaged and shot down enemy aircraft, resulting in celebration among the troops.

However, according to the U.S. military's investigation into the incident, they found no evidence of enemy planes or bombs being dropped in the area. They suspected that the U.S. Coast Guard had mistaken a weather balloon for an enemy aircraft, likely due to the heightened fear and tension stemming from the earlier bombardment of Ellwood.

Today, conspiracy theorists have speculated that this incident was an attack on the United States by extraterrestrial forces. However, most historians regard this event as a case of mass paranoia and a false alarm.

Operation Fu-Go

Operation Fu-Go was an attack on the continental United States and Canada by the Japanese Imperial Army in 1944.

Fu-Go bombs, 1942

An revenge attack

In April 1942, the U.S. Air Force initiated the Doolittle Raid as retaliation for the Japanese attack on Pearl Harbor. Subsequently, the Japanese planned a retaliatory strike on the United States. In 1942, Nobuo Fujita, a Japanese pilot unable to participate in the Pearl Harbor attack, flew to the Siskiyou National Forest and dropped two incendiary bombs in an attempt to start a widespread fire. However, local authorities quickly extinguished it. Nonetheless, it demonstrated the potential for a fire-bombing campaign against the United States. The Imperial Japanese Army assigned General Sueki Kusaba the task of building a balloon-powered fire-bomb. In March 1943, his team succeeded in constructing a 20-foot explosive device capable of remaining airborne for up to 30 hours. That same year, meteorologist Hideshi Aratawa informed the Japanese Imperial Army of a strong air current blowing from Japan to the United States in early November, facilitating the delivery of the bombs. The plan was finalized.

On November 3, 1944, the Imperial Japanese Army launched 9,300 incendiary balloon bombs from Honshu with the aim of reaching the United States and starting widespread fires, thereby weakening the U.S. war effort and securing a Japanese victory. The first balloon was discovered in San Pedro, California, alerting authorities. In response, the United States kept the discovery highly confidential to prevent widespread panic among citizens.

In May 1945, Reverend Archie Mitchell was on a Sunday picnic with his pregnant wife, Elsie, and five of his Sunday school students near the *Southern Mountains* in Oregon. While he was retrieving lunch from his car, one of the children informed him that the others had found a large balloon. He instructed the child to tell the others not to touch it. Shortly afterward, he heard a loud explosion and discovered his wife and the five children dead. They became the first and only American citizens to fall victim to an enemy attack.

On May 22, the United States ended the secrecy surrounding the incident and warned the public of the potential danger posed by these balloons. Today, over 9,000 of these balloons have been discovered in both the U.S. and Canada, with some possibly still remaining unexploded. Caution is advised if encountering any of these balloons.

The Man in the Iron Mask

The Man in the Iron Mask was an unidentified prisoner in France during the reign of Louis XIV, from 1669 to 1703. His true identity remains a mystery to this day.

The Man in the Iron Mask

A masked prisoner

In 1669, the governor of the prison at Pignerol received instructions from Louis XIV's minister, the Marquis de Louvois, regarding the imminent arrival of a prisoner. Specific directives were provided regarding the treatment of this prisoner: he was to be housed in a cell with multiple doors and granted any requested food or necessities. However, guards were instructed to always conceal the prisoner's face with a black cloth, and if he ever revealed his identity, he was to be executed. Over time, various theories emerged about the prisoner's identity. Descriptions indicated that he was of noble descent, tall in stature, devoutly religious, and fond of reading.

One particularly intriguing theory posited that the Man in the Iron Mask was Louis XIV himself, and that the individual reigning on the throne was an illegitimate son of Louis's mother, Anne of Austria, and Cardinal Mazarin. However, this theory is not widely accepted. Alternative candidates have gained more credibility since the death of "The Mask" in 1703. One such candidate is Vivien de Bulonde, who was arrested in 1691 for retreating his soldiers during the Siege of Cuneo and abandoning munitions and wounded soldiers. However, news articles suggest he was released after a few months. Another candidate is Italian diplomat Ercole Antonio Mattioli, who was kidnapped in 1679 by Louis XIV's envoys after scamming him into purchasing a castle and then revealing the purchase to his enemies. However, his timeline does not align with that of the Man in the Iron Mask.

Indeed, Voltaire's theory proposing that the Man in the Iron Mask was an older, illegitimate brother of Louis XIV is one of the most compelling. According to Voltaire, this brother was captured by Louis XIV as a means to prevent any potential challenges to the throne and to maintain his own power. This theory aligns well with the circumstances surrounding the Man in the Iron Mask, as the mask itself would serve as a means of concealing the brother's identity and preventing any recognition. Louis XIV's provision of any requested food and necessities, coupled with the condition of never revealing his identity, further supports this interpretation.

In 1703, the Man in the Iron Mask passed away in the Bastille, taking his true identity with him to the grave, thereby perpetuating the mystery surrounding his existence.

Christmas Truce

The Christmas Truce was a temporary ceasefire between troops on December 24th and 25th during World War I.

Painting of the Christmas Truce

A Jolly Holiday?

In September 1914, the Germans had set up defensive positions against the French following the Battle of the Marne. For over four months, troops had been enduring the horrible conditions of the trenches. These included oversized rats that roamed the trenches for food and spread diseases, while lice spread "trench fever," characterized by headaches, fevers, and muscle pain. Additionally, the coldness of the trenches led to "trench foot," a frostbite infection affecting the soldiers' feet.

By December 24th, 1914, troops had been suffering in the trenches as Christmas approached, a time they would normally spend peacefully with their families back home. Hoping to stop hostilities, German troops started singing Christmas songs in their trenches, placing candles and decorations on Christmas trees. The French were initially puzzled by this behavior but soon began singing alongside them. A bit later, German soldiers emerged from the trenches with their hands raised. In response, men from the French side also carefully left their trenches and put their hands up. Both sides exchanged Christmas gifts, played a match of football (soccer for Canadians), showed pictures of their wives back home, reminisced about the past, conversed, and laughed at each other's jokes. However, this wasn't the case on all fronts. On the Canadian-German front, things were quite different.

Canadian troops during World War I were known for their brutality. Under Sir Robert Borden's government, over 25,000 volunteer troops were sent to Europe, as many Canadians, especially those from Quebec, opposed the draft. This meant that Canadian soldiers were not conscripted like the Germans or French but had volunteered to fight in the war.

On December 24, 1914, along the German-Canadian trenches, German troops started singing Christmas songs, hanging decorations, and placing candles. They did not hear any singing from the other side, but one German soldier left the trench with his hands up. Seeing this, Canadian troops shot him in the head, causing his body to fall back into the trench. This led to the continuation of hostilities. Authorities forced troops to resume fighting on December 26, 1914. This event would only happen once, as by December 24, 1915, the troops had become radicalized and harbored deep hatred for each other.

The Goliath

The Goliath was a tracked mine used by the Wehrmacht (German Armed Forces) during WWII.

The Goliath

Moving Terror

In 1940, a French-controlled land mine nicknamed the Crocodile Terrestre (land crocodile) was recovered by the Germans near the Seine River. Impressed by its design, the Wehrmacht commissioned the companies Borgward and Zündapp to develop a similar device. By 1942, the machine was ready for war, and it was called the Leichter Ladungsträger Goliath, commonly known as "The Goliath." Despite its name, it was quite small. Soldiers using the device were given a small remote control to operate it. By moving the joystick forward, the robot would advance, and with a simple press of a button, the Goliath would detonate.

However, multiple problems emerged with the device: the soldiers needed a line of sight to operate it, and the Goliath often got stuck in mud or fell into ditches, rendering it inoperable. Its thin armor failed to protect its internal components from gunfire, making it ineffective against enemy troops. Additionally, despite its small size, the vehicle was incredibly heavy, weighing 820 lbs., which made it difficult to move. When used in the Battle of Anzio in 1944 in Italy, the majority of Goliaths failed to detonate. Those that did, managed to cause severe damage to enemy tanks and soldiers. When the device was captured by Allied troops, they deemed it useless for military combat and discarded them.

One story of its success was in 1944 in Southern France. As the 409th Parachute Division was patrolling, they saw a small robot heading their way. The troops stopped to observe the machine, puzzled. When they tried to grab it, the device detonated, killing everyone in the division. It was the only recorded incident of a Goliath attack with such deadly results.

Today, the companies that manufactured the Goliath, Borgward and Zündapp, have both gone bankrupt (in 2022 and 1984, respectively).

Wrangel Island Mammoths

The Wrangel Island Mammoths were the last mammoths alive in human history, surviving for 3,000 years after the extinction of other mammoths.

Painting of wooly mammoths

Raging Beast

It is believed that mammoths appeared around 6 million years ago and lived alongside humans until the Holocene period. During the Last Glacial Period, about 115,000 years ago, humans began hunting mammoths for protein and used their tusks for decoration and cave art. However, around 11,700 years ago, the *Younger Dryas* period ended, leading to a warming of Earth's atmosphere, which made it gradually uninhabitable for woolly mammoths, beginning the Quaternary Extinctions.

On Wrangel Island in Siberia, due to the cold temperatures, mammoths had not gone extinct and were still thriving. This meant that around 4000 BCE, during the time of ancient Egypt, mammoths were still alive on Wrangel Island. There are two models to explain why the mammals on Wrangel Island eventually succumbed to extinction. One is the predation model, which suggests that overhunting caused their downfall. The other is the climatic model, which proposes that climate fluctuations eventually affected Wrangel Island, leading to the end of the woolly mammoths there. The forests who overtook the arctic wasteland soon led to inhospitable climates for these animals for which their fur were too warm for. They would gradually evolve to be devoid of fur like the current elephants who roam the earth today. These were the two possibilities for why Wooly mammoths were still able to thrive in Wrangel Island for a short while before also becoming extinct.

Nevertheless, the fate of the Wrangel Island mammoths resembles the tale of many extinct creatures today that succumb to over-hunting, climate change, or invasive species. Today, many laws are in place to protect endangered species from extinction. Among these are the Tristan Albatross, the Tahiti Monarch, the Celebes Crested Macaque, the Sumatran Rhinoceros, the Bawean deer, and the Iriomote cat, among many others.

These animals, just like the Wrangel Island Mammoths, are also at risk of being extinct and some of them have only been seen once before disappearing into the wild again.

The St. Augustine Monster

The St. Augustine Monster was a creature who was thought to be the carcass of a monster found on November 30, 1896 on a beach in Florida.

Dr. DeWitt standing next to monster (1896)

The Monster of St. Augustine

On a calm day of November 30, 1896, two young boys were walking barefoot on the St. Augustine beach in Florida. This is where they would discover a dead mutilated monster of about 21 feet long, 7 feet wide. They quickly reported the monster to a local naturalist, Dr. DeWitt Webb who hired multiple men and horses to drag it to the surface so that the tide didn't take it back to the sea. He would inform the scientific community of his discovery which drew widespread attention. Dr. Webb theorized that it was the carcass of a gigantic octopus which was also confirmed by his peer, American Zoologist, Dr. A. E. Verrill, who stated it was the carcass of the *Octopus Giganteus*, a "true octopus, of colossal size".

However, a year later, Dr. A. E. Verrill retracted his statement and mentioned that he was misled and that monster was actually a sperm whale. However, it did not explain look the way it did.

In 1988, a local diver named Teddy Tucker came face to face with a gigantic white blob which appeared on the beach of Bermuda. Locals were puzzled believing it was a new species of fish or a creature that hasn't been discovered. This creature was quickly nicknamed as the "Bermuda Blob" by the media. Analyzing the pictures, it fit the same description as the St-Augustine monster: it did not have any bones, firm tissues, and that it was white as soap. Scientists had no explanation for why it would look as such and could not provide any explanation. However, it all came to light in 1995. Pierce et al. (1995) analyzed samples from the 1890s and 1988 to determine the true nature of the creature.

It was concluded that these two corpses were two sperm whales who had died at sea. After they had died, they were not eaten, but were rather dissolved by the sea. It ate away their bones, removed the color of their flesh to a bare white, and threw them onto the coast of Florida and Bermuda. It was then confirmed that these creatures were not monsters or mythical creatures, but our very own sperm whales who suffered a tragic death.

The Montauk Monster

The Montauk Monster was an alleged monster speculated to have escaped from the Plum Island biological research center in New York.

Plum Island, New York

An experiment gone wrong?

In 2008, Jenna Hewitt found a terrifying animal carcass washed up on shore. It had a lynx-like appearance, reddened skin, and teeth resembling those of a Saber Tooth tiger. She posted her finding to the journal called "F-22 Raptor" which circulated a picture of it, where it jokingly called it a failed experiment from the nearby Plum Island biological research center (see picture). From then on, the narrative caught on, and people started sharing this creature who had "fled" the Plum Island center. To appease the widespread panic of the population, Larry Penny, director of Natural Resources for the town of East Hampton, speculated it was a raccoon. This was confirmed by paleontologist Darren Naish, who identified it as *Procyon lotor*, also known as the common raccoon. However, these confirmations did not quell the conspiracy theories about the animal, and the mysterious disappearance of the cadaver only led to more questions. Residents in the area claim it was never taken away and only decomposed, which led to its disappearance. However, Jenna Hewitt claimed that it did not decompose and that "some guy" took it away and put it in his backyard. However, she did not tell the media where the body was.

This creature is part of a widespread conspiracy theory about secret facilities in the United States. As these places are secret and not much information is known about their activities, it only leads to more theories about them.

Another theory that emerged was the Montauk Project, a popular conspiracy theory that speculated that the United States experimented with time travel, brainwashing, and mind control in Camp Hero, New York. However, the Montauk Monster, just like the Montauk Project, is considered a hoax, as the claims are often far-fetched and do not have any proof to back them up.

Exorcism of Roland Doe

The Exorcism of Roland Doe was an alleged exorcism in 1949 performed by priests of the Holy Roman Catholic church to remove a demon from a young boy.

Exorcism in action

A newspaper article

In 1940, in Cottage City, Maryland, there was a boy named Roland. He loved to play with toys and especially loved board games. He would be frequently visited by his aunt, Harriet, who would play with him often. On January 14, 1949, his aunt brought back with her a new board game: the Ouija board. After they played, nothing happened, and they were not haunted. Aunt Harriet returned home the following day. However, on January 15, while the family was eating dinner, they heard dripping sounds. The family went out to check the faucet, but the faucet was closed. Before bed, the family then heard scratching sounds coming from the roof. At night, it continued and became even louder. Frustrated, the family hired an exterminator to remove the rats from the roof. However, after the exterminators scoured the roof, they did not find anything.

This series of events continued until January 26. On January 26, Aunt Harriet died, and the scratching sounds stopped. At night, when Roland went to sleep, he heard a different sound. Now, instead of the scratching, he heard footsteps coming from the roof and the sounds of the squeaking roof. When he went back to school the following day, his school desk moved by itself, and the teacher told him to stop moving it. However, during the Sunday class, many of the chairs in the classroom started to rise and fall down. The teacher was shocked and could not explain the situation. When his parents heard this news, they decided to hire priests from the local church in order to stop these paranormal events, which they attributed to demons.

Exorcists came to the home of the boy. The priests started chanting prayers in Latin to the boy, during which his demeanor suddenly changed. Dark red lines started appearing on his body, marking him with the word HELL. The priests also recalled the boy starting to speak in a deep and unnatural voice. After hours of incantation, the boy relaxed, and the demon seemed to have gone away.

The story was published in a journal in 1949, which would eventually inspire the creation of the movie "The Exorcist," which recalls the same story. Today, many people are skeptical of the story, believing it is merely a tale or that the child was suffering from a mental illness, acting the way he did.

Cases of Blood Rain

Ein erschrockliches Wunderzeichen zu Dinckelspühel
geschehen am Sambstag nach Vrbani des M. D. LIIII. Jars.

Anno Domini M. D. LIIII. am
Sambstag nach Vrbani / welches war
der xxvj. tag Maij / hat es zu Dinckel=
spühel warhafftig blut geregnet / zwischē
xj. vnnd xij. der kleynen vhr vmb mittag /
vnnd hat sich erstlich also erfunden. Ein
fraw hat jr wesch vor dem Thor auffge=
hangen / hembd / leylach / vnd tischtücher /
Do ist die wesch vol mit bluts tropffen
gefallen / vnd als sie das wider hat auß=
waschen wöllen / ist es noch röter worden.
Als sie erschrocken ist vnd das gesagt hat /
hat das volck erst wargenumen / das das
blut hin vnd wider auff die baum / büsch /
vñ zeun gefallē ist gewesen. Vnd haben
solcher bletter zu einem wunder in vil an=
dere Stet ein guter freunde dem andern
zugeschickt. Vrsach solches blut regens /
weiß Gott allein / Wiewol es on zweyffel
ein erschröckliches warzeichen ist / krieg
vñ blutvergiessens / wie das denn allemal
auff solch blutregnen gefolget hat / Gott
wende es zum besten / vnd geb vns seinen
heyligen Geyst inn vnser hertz / puß zu
thun / von vnsern vilfeltigen sünden / von
welcher wegen / der Gottes zorn ob vns
angangen ist vnnd prinnt / Gott wöll vns
gnedig vnd barmhertzig sein / Amen.

Gedruckt zu Nürnberg durch Hans Glaser /

Blood rain depicted in a 1554 publication

One of the mysterious phenomena in history is blood rain. It can be found in many primary sources and has happened in modern times as well. These are the main events we know of:

181 BCE: On the evening of 181 BCE, Titus Livy, a Roman historian, was leaving his house when blood-colored rain fell upon him. It was such in all of Rome. Officials entered a state of panic as blood rain was considered a bad omen. They hosted a sacrifice ceremony and sacrificed multiple animals in order to end the blood rain. However, the rain did not stop for several hours.

685 CE: Hlothhere, king of Kent, founder of the legal codes of Hlothhere, was sick and felt that he was going to die soon. Right when he felt he was going to die, he saw blood rain trickle from the window. Shortly after, he died. Outside,

people reported that butter and milk were turned into blood. Some attributed the event to the death of their king.

1198 CE: An unnamed king reported that during combat, blood rain poured from the sky and tainted his soldiers' clothes and his armor. It scared both sides of the troops, and both went back home, postponing the battle for another time.

1957 CE: On that day, blood rain poured from the sky in India. From the analysis of the blood sample, the CCE determined that it was not blood but water containing heavy metals like chromium or titanium. It was initially suspected to be caused by a meteor, but it was then attributed to airborne spores.

2001 CE: Blood rain poured again in Kerala, India. Following the incident, scientists decided to re-investigate the issue and attributed the coloring of the particles because of aerial spores of the *Trentepohlia annulata*.

2024 CE: Just like the king of Kent received in England, Britain is expected to receive blood rain on January 29, 2024, which comes from the Saharan Dust Plume. At the time of writing this article (January 29), it is still unclear whether Britain will be tainted with it.

The Life of General Villa (1914)

"The Life of General Villa" is a lost movie filmed in 1914 by General Pancho Villa, a Mexican revolutionary.

Pancho Villa in 1916

Movie of the Dead

In 1910, a civil war broke out when Mexican dictator Porfirio Diaz retook power after announcing his retirement. After organizing free elections, he jailed one of the most popular competitors in the Mexican political sphere, Francisco Madero. From then on, multiple leaders emerged to support Madero, including Emiliano Zapata, Pascual Orozco, Venustiano Carranza, and Pancho Villa. Pancho Villa rose to become a notorious power in the South and was nicknamed the Mexican Robin Hood because of his habit of robbing trains and establishments and giving to the poor. During his time, he became quite popular in the United States, known for his exploits and his large sombrero. Needing money to fund his army, he exploited that fame to some money.

In 1914, he signed a contract with Mutual Film Company to make a movie about himself, hoping it would sell well at the box office and earn him some money for the war. After signing the contract, he received $350,000 from the Mutual Film Company for them to film and direct the movie. They filmed a couple of scenes in the beginning with his mother, while the rest of the scenes followed Pancho Villa. However, when the filming was finished, it was unpopular with the directors, and they vomited during the screening. Allegedly, the scenes contained shootings involving actual soldiers being shot dead, villagers looting corpses and removing golden fillings from soldiers' teeth, and real execution scenes. The movie was considered a total flop, and the directors decided not to release it to the public.

After the movie was scrapped, they decided not to give up and made another movie called "The Property Man," which starred Charlie Chaplin and for which he was paid $670,000 a year.

The movie became widely popular, which led to lots of revenue for Charlie. Meanwhile, for Pancho Villa, things weren't going so well. He had been by Venustiano Carranza in the *Battle of Agua Prieta* in 1915 and lost most of his troops. His defeat was mostly due that Carranza was funded by the United States. Hence, Villa would then lead a punitive expedition against the United States in the *Battle of Columbus,* which led to the destruction of a town in Mexico. It would lead to a hunt for Pancho Villa by the U.S. which led to nothing as they were not able to capture him. Pancho Villa would finally retire in 1920. He would be assassinated three years later*.

White Wilderness Controversy

The White Wilderness controversy was a filming controversy involving Disney 1958 nature documentary, *White Wilderness.*

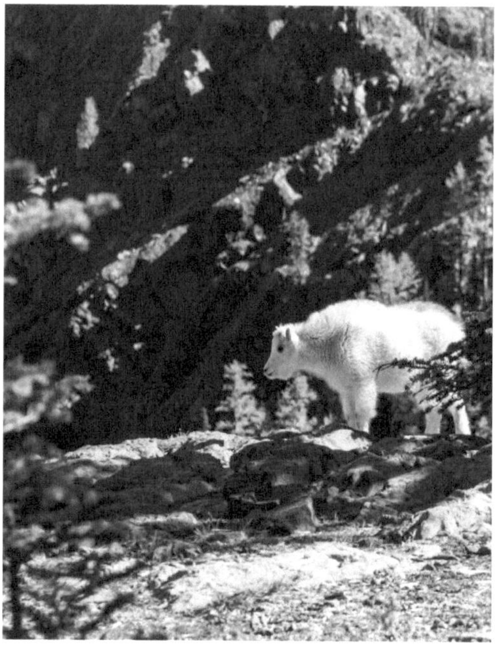

Dying Lemur

White Wilderness was a 1958 documentary which came into addition to Disney's *True-Life Adventures* series, a non-fiction nature documentary series. It was the last in many of the series, including its vastly successful *Seal Island* in 1948, which won best documentary award. In 1954, they would film the vastly successful *The Living Desert,* focused on the lives of the animals and insects in the desert and *The Vanishing Prairie* in 1955, focused on the living things of the prairies. One of its last installments of the series was *White Wilderness,* where it focused its series on the animals of the North American arctic. However, everything would go wrong for the series in 1982, where a Canadian program, the *Fifth Estate*, would investigate the movie once more as part of their *Cruel Camera* series, which worked to investigate animal abuse within the filming industry. In it, they had discovered that the majority of *The Living Desert* was fake and multiple scenes were filmed within a studio and scorpions were filmed within a small enclosure and edited to look like they were out in the wild. However, the biggest revelation was on *White Wilderness*. In one part of the movie, the narrator, Winston Hibbler, announced that lemmings were susceptible to be "victims of obsession" and to cast themselves into the sea. However, it was a made-up lie. In fact, the director, James Algar, had filmed the scene in Alberta, Canada, of which he used a machine to propel snow in order to throw the lemmings off a cliff to make it look like a natural death. But as a matter of fact, it was quite the opposite, creating the long-standing myth that lemmings were susceptible to mass-suicide.

As well, the series had also faked multiple scenes, notably one scene where a baby polar bear fell from an icecap which was filmed in a film studio in Vancouver, Canada. Another scene that was filmed was Canadian geese flying within the skies, of which it was later discovered that the geese were tied to a roof in a film studio and fans flew on the geese to simulate wind. In response, the film directors would claim that the geese enjoyed flying, and it did not hurt them.

The documentary would expose the dark and grueling truth in nature documentaries, where many scenes are often staged for the sake of the movie. As well, in 2020, after the release of Disney's premium streaming software, *Disney +*, *White Wilderness* would briefly appear in the list of watchable movies before being removed permanently. It is currently only available on YouTube.

Dyatlov Pass Incident

The Dyatlov Pass Incident was an incident in which nine hikers between February 1-9, 1957 would succumb to an unknown force.

Tent where the hikers disappeared

Frozen Wasteland

On October 4, 1957, Soviet scientists managed to launch Sputnik-I, the first satellite into space, beating the Americans spinning a vast amount of pride within the Soviet Union. To emphasize on the Soviet Union's success, Igor Dyatlov, an inventor and student of the Ural Polytechnic Institute (UPI) would host a 17 day long *Winter Expedition* alongside other students into the Ural Mountains to demonstrate the fierceness and persistence of the people of the Soviet Union. The request for the trip was quickly granted. On January 28th, he and his members, seven men and two women headed out to the Ural mountains to the expedition.

Amongst them were experienced skiers, athletes of which all of them had the minimum requirement of being a *Grade-II* hiker which was required for the expedition. However, it is believed that on February 1-9 of 1957, they were all killed by unknown forces. On February 20th, after worried outcries by university teachers and family members, several search parties were launched in order to uncover what had happened to the students. On February 25th, in an area called the *Dead Mountains*, police would find all nine students.

Upon finding their tent, they saw the tent was cut from inside and that many of the students fled on barefoot and at the bottom of the cliff, they saw two students surrounded by a dead fire in their underwear, frozen to death. Further down the cliff, they found two other students, both in similar conditions, but this time, one student had blackened fingers and had ripped out a part of his arm as his flesh was still within his teeth when he was found.

A couple of days later, the rest of the bodies were found. Two of the bodies had their eyes removed with both of their chest crushed and the last student had a heavy dent in her skull of which pieces of her brain were found near her body. This triggered a homicide investigation of which they eventually determined that "*they had succumbed to a powerful force of which they were unable to overcome*".

Over the years, many theories have emerged, including the Yeti theory, of which an ancient Beast had tracked and attacked them or the Soviet test of which the students were victims of a secret Soviet weapon. However, the leading theory today was that the students had succumbed to an avalanche leading them to flee or to be crushed by the avalanche.

Polybius

Polybius was an urban legend about an arcade machine in 1981 that purportedly could cause night terrors, hallucinations, insomnia, amnesia, and more.

Alleged Polybius arcade

A new MK-Ultra?

In 1981, in Portland, Oregon, residents allegedly noticed new arcade machines placed all around the city. It was called Polybius. In the game, players assumed the role of Polybius (named after the Greek historian) and had to shoot at enemy players, leading to large flashes from explosions and psychedelic effects. Some residents reported feeling nauseous, experiencing hallucinations, and suffering from insomnia after playing the game. According to the podcast "The Polybius Conspiracy", one man named Bobby Feldstein claimed that in 1981, while he was playing the game, he felt strange and was then abducted. He recalls being led into a dark and wide tunnel and then blacking out before waking up in the Tillamook State Forest, where he had to trek 60 miles to get home. From then on, many suspected that Polybius was a product of the U.S. government's Project MK-Ultra, to test the effect of the machine's psychoactive properties. However, one month later, the machines disappeared.

In the early 2000s, rumors of this event still circulated on the internet. However, the tale of it changed drastically, and multiple versions of the story emerged. Some stories claimed that Polybius brainwashed children into becoming soldiers for the United States, while others said it was a regular maze game or space shooter. Some stories also stated that children, after playing the game, experienced night terrors and amnesia. Today, it is widely accepted that the game was an urban legend and that it never existed.

However, the urban legend inspired many people, such as Ernest Cline, a young author who heard about it in the early 2000s. It inspired him to write a science fiction novel called "Ready Player One," in which the protagonist plays a virtual reality game to find an Easter egg left by the game's creator in order to inherit his fortune. Cline published the book in 2011, and it quickly became a New York Times bestseller. It was also adapted into a movie in 2018.

Additionally, it inspired classics like "The Last Starfighter" (1984), where a young boy is recruited by aliens because of his exceptional gaming skills, and "Nightmares" (1983), where a level called "The Battle of Bishop" is so addictive that it absorbs the player into the game.

Volkswagen Diesel Scandal

The Volkswagen Diesel Scandal was a 2015 global scandal involving Volkswagen, which caused a 16-billion-dollar lawsuit by the U.S. Government.

Volkswagen Jetta, Green Car of the Year (2009)

A rigged car?

In 2013, the U.S. government required all cars to pass standard emission test (SETs) in order to approve the cars for sale in the United States. When the Volkswagen Jetta and Volkswagen Passat passed the test, it was shown that their emissions were well below the emission levels, which got them approved and also recognized as a "clean car" for the environment. However, in 2015, Volkswagen was discovered to have had a "defeat device" at the bottom of vehicles that could detect when they were being tested and reduce emissions during tests. When the Volkswagen was tested without the defeat device, it was shown that Volkswagen had been producing over 40 times the allowed amount. Soon, scandal emerged and caused Volkswagen to buy back a large amount of their cars and settle a lawsuit with the United States for violating environmental laws and releasing a large amount of NO2 into the atmosphere. In April 2016, they would receive over $14.7 billion in fines by the U.S. Government.

More damning, in May 2015, the company allegedly tested their vehicles on ten Java monkeys in Mexico, of which they were locked in an airtight box, forced to breathe in the fumes of a Volkswagen beetle. Then, they would breathe in the fumes of a Ford F-150 who did not have a filter like the beetle. The experiment consisted of trying to prove that the smoke from the Beetle was not that harmful to humans, but instead the monkeys suffered severe respiratory problems and the results were discarded until it resurfaced again.

In response to the scandal, Volkswagen had initially denied the allegations of a "defeat device", but would be ultimately forced to admit it. Multiple members of Volkswagen, including prominent officials and engineers who had developed the defeat device, would be subsequently arrested. The stock price of the Volkswagen would drastically fall as well, and the trust in Volkswagen would never recover.

Today, Volkswagen had accumulated over $33 M dollars in fines as of June 2020.

Cicada 3301

Cicada 3301 was an internet mystery that emerged on 4chan, where anonymous users attempted to find "the smartest individuals in the world."

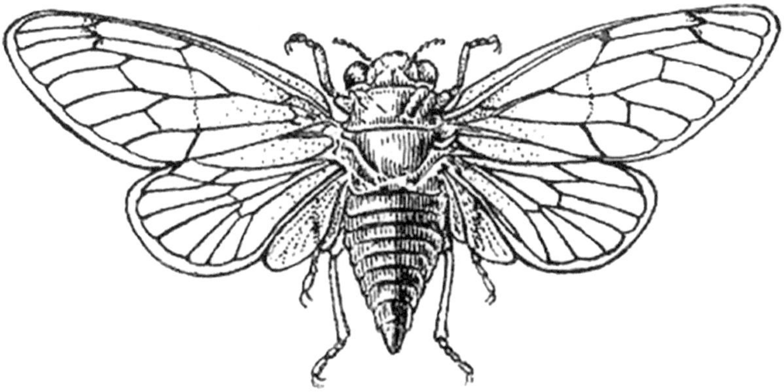

Cicada logo

A treasure hunt

In 2012, an anonymous user posted a message on 4chan that puzzled users. In a white background with the picture of a Cicada, it read:

> *"Hello. We are looking for highly intelligent individuals. To find them, we have devised a test. There is a message hidden in this image. Find it, and it will lead you on the road to finding us. We look forward to meeting the few that will make it all the way through. Good luck."*

Even though the post was ignored by many as a fraud, some users were particularly interested in finding out the puzzle. In the first picture of the Cicada, some individuals realized that the PNG image was actually a Shift Cypher which led them to a URL directing them to the picture of a duck with the text:

"WHOOPS, Just decoys your way." Upon decoding the cypher, the users would discover that it led to a Reddit user called a2e7j6ic78h0j7eiejd0120, who posted multiple encoded messages inside of it. The next series of puzzles led them to understand how Mayan numbers work and how cicadas migrate to decode the entire puzzle. After several other puzzles, users were led to a series of GPS coordinates containing physical letters to solve their puzzle. Clues were found in Miami, Warszawa, Paris, Erskineville, and Fayetteville. Only a few were able to solve this puzzle, and their fate is unknown. These puzzles would eventually lead each individual to a specific site. Nothing was known afterwards. It is believed that Cicada 3301 might have been a recruitment operation by the NSA, while some believed it was a recruiting effort by a hacking group.

It is also believed that Cicada 3301 was a mere ploy by an intelligent individual who simply wanted to receive some attention and built an entire puzzle to get people to solve and figure out.

In 2014, a new series of Cicada puzzles were posted, but they haven't garnered as much success as the first one and the puzzle was never solved.

KFK Time Traveller

On June 22, 2019, a Chinese user on *Douban* claimed to have experienced time travel, sparking intrigue among netizens who bombarded him with questions about the future.

Douban offices

A visitor from the future

On June 22 of 2019, a post titled *"I'm a time-traveler, ask me anything"* was posted by a user called *@kfk* on Douban. In response, many users called him a fraud, but some began believing he was a time traveler. One notable prediction involved the 2020 United States presidential election, where the alleged time traveler foresaw Donald Trump's victory during the election despite the massive belief that the former president would lose the election. In response, many users did not believe @kfk and he would post multiple other predictions that would come true. For example, he would also predict that Tsai Ing-wen would win the elections in Taiwan and that controversies would emerge in the 2020 Tokyo Olympics. As well, he would add a series of very precise predictions to show his followers that he was serious, that he had developed a time-machine.

2019: Major world-wide incident
2022: Incident involving Taiwan's return to China.
2032: Olympics held at Jakarta
2035: World's first holographic games involving taste
2038: China's entrance exam abolished
2038: Robots widely used, just like cell phones
2048: Homosexuality legalized in China
2049-2051: A series of global wars emerge
2051-2060: Collective suffering in a post-war period 2060: Civilization slowly rebuilds, houses are quickly built.
2060: Bitcoin ceases to exist

He explained that in 2060, he had developed a time-machine to allow him to teleport to 2019, a year before his birth, to send a message. However, on November 6 of 2020, @kfk lost the entirety of his credibility after Donald J. Trump lost the elections to the former vice-president, Joseph R. Biden.

Today, the user is nowhere to be seen, but it is believed that the user is still on the platform, but this time, choosing to not make any more posts.

Gamergate

Gamergate was an organized misogynistic hate campaign between 2014-2015, leading several women to suffer from post-traumatic stress disorder (PTSD).

Zoë Quinn in 2015

#Gamergate

In 2014, a post titled "the Zoë Post" began a widespread harassment campaign against predominant female game developers, content creators, and activists. In the post, it alleged that Zoë had slept with a game reviewer from Kotaku and Rock Paper Shotgun to get positive reviews for their game, *Depression Quest.* Following the allegations, Zoë would receive a massive amount of death threats, r*pe threats as well as receiving threatening phone calls from users who had coordinated via IRC (internet relay chat) and met on Reddit or 4chan. Redditors also coordinated attacks such as doxing, hacking and even sending nude pictures of her to her dad or her colleagues. Throughout the experience, she was deeply traumatized and afraid for her life, giving her symptoms of post-traumatic stress disorder (PTSD). It was later found out that the allegations were made up by her ex-boyfriend, Eron Gjoni. Thought it all, he had suddenly sparked an online crusade who began waging against feminism, gender equality and social "wokeness" in video games, which they viewed as the downfall of gaming.

Another victim of Gamergate would be Anita Sarkeesian, who animated a series called *Women Vs Tropes in Video Games,* which broke down the various misogynistic tropes in games. In response to her work, Gamergate activists harassed her and published death threats, rape threats, and doxed her address. As well, Gamergaters promoted the idea of committing a mass-shooting like the Montreal Polytechnique Massacre at the Utah State University where she would have a conference. She would soon cancel her tour there and hide.

Brianna Wu, a fellow activist and game developer was also a target of Gamergate in mid-2014. She was given rape threats, death threats as well as Gamergaters calling anyone who came to her defense as "social justice warriors" or "white knights". Two members of Gamergate also tried to instigate a SWAT raid on her which could have potentially killed her, but the emergency services were aware of the situation and did not call a SWAT team at her home.

Through it all, it caused a vast amount of trauma, fear, and has shown the disgusting misogynistic side of the internet that stills rules today.

Section II:
Violence

The next pages may contain some **shocking images or content** (either hidden in the embed links or in the general picture). Please read with caution.